Cryptocurrency Trading from Beginner to Advanced

Proven Strategies to Make Money Day Trading Crypto Assets like Bitcoin Using Charting, Technical Analysis, and Psychology

Jim Hoffer

Table of Contents

Introduction

The crypto market is still in its nascent stage as most regulators are still setting up ways to monitor the trade of cryptocurrencies and make it easier for new investors to dip their feet in the pond. This makes such assets the ideal thing to invest in because the competition still hasn't enlarged to a point where you can't enter the market at all. As a new investor, cryptocurrencies are the ideal assets to trade if you can just get beyond the technical complications. The biggest barrier for most people is that they don't have the technical know-how required to enter this market – the purpose of this book is to bridge precisely this gap. Even finding the right exchange can be quite difficult, but once you know what the most reliable networks to depend upon are, the return you will experience will ensure that all the hard work was worth it.

The biggest advantage crypto assets have for new investors is that they're extremely volatile. Now, this can be both a good thing and a bad thing, but if you know what you're doing, you can pretty much ensure that you get huge returns on the smallest of your investments. For example, Bitcoin's value has been so volatile that it has become quite a cultural joke. Its price can increase or decrease at a ginormous rate in just a few months.

On the other hand, there are currencies whose prices are much more stable, so if you are not someone who likes taking risks, this is the direction you should head in. But, the volatility of this market is what draws people in – the rags to riches story that has been popularized because Bitcoin acts in a way that amplifies people's interest in this new commodity. This can also be your story, but only if you know what you're doing – once you have researched the market properly, then you'll be able to make decisions that are far sounder than just throwing money and hoping you get the returns you dreamed of.

This market also never sleeps, as opposed to most fiat currencies that governments regulate. The crypto market is available twenty-four hours a day. You can even trade with individuals, an option you don't have with other markets. The benefits of cryptocurrencies are:

Most cryptocurrencies are decentralized and are not controlled by any nation or business.

There is no central point of failure, so if one organization mining Bitcoins or other major cryptocurrencies fails, then the currency continues

The use of cryptocurrencies allows much greater privacy than the use of fiat currencies

Cryptocurrencies are very easy to use, often much easier than fiat currencies which require time and fees for transactions

Transfers using cryptocurrency are much quicker than fiat

For merchants, there is no danger of chargeback where a disgruntled customer can void a transaction that used a credit card

Due to their electronic form, cryptocurrencies are far more durable and portable than fiat money

As a result of cryptography, the chance of fraud is far less than fiat, with credit card numbers routinely hacked and put on the Internet

Are you scared of missing out on trading cryptocurrencies? This book is a way to help you trade cryptocurrencies quickly. Let's look at a quick plan to help you trade in cryptocurrencies:

Understand if you only want to trade the currency or want to own it. It is also important to know the values of the currencies that will go up or down:

You need to look at an exchange if you want to own the currency. You can use BitMex, which is a user-friendly and simple application. Having said that, it is important to do your due diligence, so you know which exchange is best for you.

If you only want to use the price to your advantage, finding a broker to help you is best. Learn about the brokers you can connect with and who does best in the cryptocurrency market before you choose them to take care of your money.

Fund the account and add the amount you want to trigger or invest

If you want the cryptocurrency, you should buy it and then open a trade on the price of that currency

You are officially a cryptocurrency trader. Bear in mind that you can practice the strategies and run the entire purchase and sale of the currency through a demo account if needed. It is unfortunate that you cannot practice trading cryptocurrencies on an exchange. When it comes to trading cryptocurrencies, you need to speculate the price and volatility of the currency. You do not have to own the coins. For this reason, CFDs and forex are easier to invest in, especially if you are a beginner. This is the alternative of buying the currency through a cryptocurrency exchange.

This book aims to provide information about what cryptocurrencies are and how they can be traded. But before we dive into that, we will look at the different ways the human mind affects your decision-making. This is something you must be aware of since most decisions you make are based on emotional responses, and this is something you need to avoid when it comes to trading any stock.

It is, however, extremely important to set your emotions aside when you trade cryptocurrencies since they are extremely volatile. These virtual coins have reached a new price in the last decade. Many crypto coins were introduced in the market, and most of the popular cryptocurrency exchange platforms had seen an increase in their user base.

Many investors have also been trying to learn more about investing in cryptocurrencies because they can make a lot of money through virtual currencies. Unfortunately, many investors are rushing in because they do not want to miss out on the benefits without understanding what exactly needs to be done when investing in cryptocurrencies. This is causing a lot of them to fail when they begin trading.

It is important to understand that cryptocurrencies are still in their nascent stages, and they are highly volatile currencies. While some of these currencies, like Bitcoin and others, are a substitute for different stocks and securities in the market, bear in mind that the market for trading cryptocurrencies is smaller when compared to the stock and security market.

If you choose to invest in cryptocurrencies, understand that the investing methods and strategies are very different from stock market strategies. If you choose to invest in cryptocurrencies, it is important to understand the currencies well. You need to understand the technology being used and the coin's market value before you invest. Since cryptocurrencies are volatile, it becomes imperative to understand how to trade in them despite their price fluctuations.

In this book, you will gather information about cryptocurrencies and how you should invest in them. Before we dive into that, we will understand how an investor thinks and the different biases that make him hedge his bets and take risks. It is important for you to understand these biases so you do not ruin your chances of making a profit. If you are a beginner, you can use this book to guide you on the various trading strategies used in cryptocurrency trading. The book also has some tips on how to trade some of the most popular cryptocurrencies.

Use the information in this book to help you make the right decisions. Do not let your emotions guide you because that is only going to lead you to failure. It is important to understand that you are bound to make mistakes. Do not let those mistakes deter you. You need to learn from those mistakes and do everything needed to ensure you have an airtight strategy. You can use various platforms to help you test the strategies and do everything you can to improve those strategies. It is important to have a large risk capital, so you can overcome any losses you make.

Thank you for purchasing the book. I hope you learn everything you need to about cryptocurrency trading and implement the techniques accurately.

Chapter One: Trading Psychology

Trading psychology refers to the emotional and mental state of a trader, which helps to decide the extent of their success or failure in the market. It showcases several aspects of the character and behavior of a trader. It can also help one understand why a trader incurred heavy losses.

Trading psychology is critical in judging the trading performance of a trader as well as other important qualities such as awareness, knowledge, ability as a trader, the amount of experience in the field, etc.

Trading psychology is subjective as it is under the influence of each individual's own emotions and biases. Some emotions and gut feelings are helpful, while other feelings such as greed, fear, nervousness, anxiety, etc., can immensely affect the success rate of a trader. The main idea behind learning about trading psychology is to become aware of the several disadvantages experienced due to a negative psychological trait and develop more positive traits.

Traders who have an understanding of trading psychology will generally avoid acting on emotions and biases and will make an informed decision. This helps them stand a better chance of earning a profit during their time in the markets or at least minimizing their losses.

Traders are constantly in competition with other traders as well as with themselves. As humans, they want their egos to be validated. They want to prove to themselves and others that they are well aware of their steps. They also want to survive in the market. All these emotions taken together can lead to losses until and unless we learn to control them.

Leading Emotions Faced by Traders:

Fear

Fear is basically pain or loss avoidance. It is a major emotion that a trader has to deal with in reaction to a perceived threat.

If a trader had lost money in the past, they would normally associate those painful trades with the current market state, so the fear they experience is self-generated.

When you make a trade, you expect the market to move in the direction beneficial to you. Fear starts affecting the trader when the movement is in the opposite direction instead.

Fear sometimes freezes us. A trader might not be able to invest in a profitable opportunity because they may be suffering fear or trauma from past failures and may hesitate to take a position. Some common situations where fear affects the trader are:

Not investing in a trade due to the fear that they might not get it right and end up losing.

Not selling a losing trade because if the price starts increasing, they will suffer a loss.

Selling too soon, fearing that they will lose profits.

Greed

Greed is a desire for immense profits. It is a tricky emotion because the traders are in the markets to earn profits.

How much profit is too much profit? If the markets are performing in congruence with their expectations, why should they consider leaving the position? Why not make more profits?

Greed forces us to consider these questions. This is more common in a bullish market when the prices are high. Traders hold on to their winning positions longer than advisable and are grasped by greed.

Each trader must identify and ensure that they do not cross the thin line between greed and optimism.

Hope

Hope is a positive emotion sans any logic and can therefore lead to substantial losses. It is the one thing that separates trading from gambling.

Traders must learn how to control being too hopeful because hope can destroy their capital if not managed. Greed attached to hope can lead to fatal problems for a trader's career.

Biases

Acting on their emotions and ego, traders can commit certain biases. Here mentioned are a few prominent biases:

Overconfidence Bias

As committed by traders, this bias is composed of two components: overconfidence in the quality of the information they have and their ability to act on that information at the appropriate time to maximize profits.

It is a tendency to have an inflated assessment of your skills or talent. An overconfident trader becomes very prone to making mistakes. Overconfidence promotes traders to be insufficiently cautious in trading decisions. They have an illusion of control and think they have good control over the situation when they do not.

Overconfident traders can get themselves into trouble by placing unusually large trades or also by trading too frequently. This creates huge risk, and there are high chances of the trade going bad. An inaccurate assessment of risk leads to failure.

Anchoring Bias

Anchoring bias is the tendency to believe that the future is going to look quite similar to the present. It occurs when traders rely too much on the first information they get or find while making trading decisions.

Anchors are often involved while trading in currencies, as those are intrinsically hard to value. The degree of anchoring is dependent on how important the anchor is. More traders cling to a relevant anchor.

Anchored traders convince themselves that the ongoing trend will never end, and a reversal in the economic strength is almost impossible.

Confirmation Bias

The propensity of traders to pay attention only to the information that confirms the belief that they already have is known as confirmation bias. The traders do not pay heed to any information that is in contradiction to their beliefs.

Confirmation bias limits the trader's ability to make purely rational decisions. They miss the important warning signs that generally would have protected them from incurring losses. The traders miss the facts while building a case for their beliefs. Eventually, they lose profits with each ill-conceived trade.

Representativeness Bias

Traders usually make the mistake of believing that similar events are correlated, but that isn't always true. This is called representativeness bias.

The trader must understand that chart patterns are only a record of past market movements that suggest that the chances of the market moving in a particular direction is slightly larger. There is a considerable probability that the chart pattern prediction may not pan out. Therefore, it is important that the trader sets specific parameters to exit the trade ideas that are not working. A chart pattern does not guarantee that the price will go up. Any trader actually trading according to the chart patterns without any risk management may be preparing for a failure.

Overcoming Biases

Good traders can be identified by the manner in which they handle their emotions and biases. A trading market is an exceptionally competitive environment, and therefore, a trader must learn to control their emotions or have a poor chance of becoming a successful trader.

Here are some methods to overcome psychological trading biases:

Create a Trading Plan

In order to overcome bias, a trader must plan his trade beforehand and not when the trade is initiated. Trading in a haphazard way might lead to loss of capital. If they want consistent profits, traders must create a trading plan and stick to it. They should also have a contingency plan set if things start to go down.

Focus on Research

Traders must undertake trades according to the information based on solid market research and data. They should not believe in market rumors as they generally lead to capital losses.

Be on the Lookout for Contrary Data

Traders tend to look for and believe in views that match their own. The trading decision must be taken with complete objectivity, and they must obtain and consider resources that look at the same events differently.

Take Responsibility

A trader must have a clear goal in mind and should also learn to be accountable for his trades. They should deal with criticism and any sort of feedback with a positive mindset.

Stay Humble

Traders should not translate a few trading successes into pride and arrogance. This can lead to capital destruction in the long run.

Understand Yourself

A trader often experiences extreme emotions only during a winning or losing streak. These emotions must be taken into account so that they can be worked upon and psychological biases can be overcome.

Why Do Traders Need a New Thinking Methodology?

The typical social way an individual is raised with certain beliefs and values is incompatible with the methods needed to be successful in the trading environment. Someone believing that they will always get what they want will constantly find themselves in a state of frustration because their belief will be inconsistent with the results.

In trading, success will always seem so close but yet so distant. Therefore, this frustration will continue to inconvenience the trader until they learn to adapt to the conditions of the market. They can do this by learning and developing for themselves completely new thinking methods. A thinking methodology that will prove effective in the trading environment and is not based solely on their cultural upbringing is very likely to reduce the burden of feeling like a failure every time there is a loss.

A beginner in the trading market is faced with a very different environment from anything they have experienced before. The ever-changing market, no security of success, unlimited potential for profit and loss, the perpetual news of other traders winning and losing, all of this is what trading looks like every day, every moment. Humans have gone far and beyond to create specific structures, define boundaries, set limits, etc., to their lifestyle choices so that things remain static. An unchanged and steady environment is what people are used to because that is what makes them feel secure and comfortable.

The markets can knock down this sense of security by actively forcing the trader to go through continuous change every moment. This will create an environment that is emotionally depleting, stressful, and extremely competitive. The markets are capable of satisfying a trader's grandest and wildest dreams and, at the same time, can take away everything they own. There is an overwhelming need to win millions alongside the fear of being financially destroyed.

To add to the emotional and mental burden, trading does not work according to the principles of time, effort, and reward, the elements that are primarily existent in most jobs. Effort is totally irrelevant to a trader, and there is no amount of time they can spend to ensure success. Even making a lot of money in a matter of minutes or seconds can lead to a mental conflict because of the general belief that effort and reward should be directly proportional.

The dissonances between the cultural and market environments must be adjusted by adopting a thinking methodology better suited for the trading world. This can help a trader understand market behavior and reduce mistakes by not letting their emotions come in the way of undertaking trading-related decisions.

Socially and Culturally Learned Behavior That Results in Committing Mistakes While Trading

In the trading world that calls for split-second decision-making, there is hardly any time to compare the ongoing event with previous trade experiences. It would not even be noticeable if you had made such decisions in the past and suffered similar devastating consequences. Typical reactions can lead to failure. Recognizing them can prevent you from having to suffer losses.

Following are some typical errors commonly committed by traders. Their causes are embedded in a thinking methodology that can be changed for good.

Not defining a loss.

Not dissolving or liquidating a trade even when it has lost all its potential to create profits.

Keeping an unchanged view about market direction.

Not acting on your instincts.

Revenge trading or trying to get back at the market for the losses you incurred because of your decisions.

Always focusing only on the monetary value of a trade.

Maintaining a static position, even when there is an obvious change in the market direction.

Putting your winnings back in the market every time you experience success in trading.

Not following the rules of the trading system.

Skills to Be Acquired

In order to excel in any activity, we need to learn specialized skills. To succeed in trading, you need the skills of thought application. One such skill is the ability to recognize conditions that lead to making common mistakes in trading. Other techniques are:

Learning the components of goal achievement in order to stay positive and focused on what you want and not on what you fear.

Do not make money the center of your attention. It is merely a by-product of your skills as a trader. Learning how to identify and acknowledge the skills you need to grow as a trader and stay focused on developing and achieving those skills.

Learning how to adjust in response to the dynamic changes in the market.

Organizing your beliefs to control your impression of market conditions.

Measuring and identifying the quota of risk you are comfortable with.

Learning how to expand your risk comfort level in a way that you can still keep an objective view of market activity.

Learning how to attain and maintain a state of being totally objective.

Planning for the immediate execution of your trades as soon as you perceive an opportunity.

Not assessing the potential of a trade according to your own value system and instead letting the market do it for you.

Learning to recognize verifiable intuitive information.

The nature of the trading environment from a psychological perspective

The market is always right

If, while trading, you ever think that you are right and the market is wrong, the reality of the situation is that you are wrong. The market is never wrong.

The market is not going to reward your process just because your analysis and processes have been correct. It all depends on the outcome.

The market is just what it is. It is always right. It is the constant benchmark against which you are going to measure.

There Is Unlimited Potential For Profit and Loss

In any trade, you never know how far the prices will go. If you do not know where the market may stop, it is very easy to think and create a belief that there are no limits to how much profit you can earn on any given trade.

Developing such a belief will allow you to indulge in the illusion that every trade carries the potential of fulfilling all your dreams and fantasies. Let's say you believe that the market participants (buyers and sellers) can act as a force great enough to move prices in your direction. In that case, you will gather only the kind of information that will reinforce your belief while losing vital information that may be telling you the best opportunity is in the opposite direction.

The belief in the possibility of unlimited profits is extremely dangerous. It will be a huge obstacle keeping you from learning how to make a decision from an objective perspective.

Prices Are in Perpetual Motion

The market never stops - it is always in motion. As long as there are traders who are willing to buy higher and traders who are willing to sell lower than the last price, the market will keep moving.

The three simple decisions - enter, hold or liquidate a trade - becomes a never-ending process of deciding how much profit or loss is enough.

If you are getting profits from your trade, is it ever enough? The appetite for greed can never be satisfied. If you were in a losing trade, you would convince yourself that things have not worked out in your favor yet and continue trading.

The market can always tempt you and make you feel that you can have more in a winning trade. It can also give you something to hang on to in a losing trade so that you are hopeful that it will come back and make you whole. Giving in to either one of these temptations can lead to disastrous consequences.

The Market Is an Unstructured Environment

The market has a constant flow, with no beginning or end. It has no structure. It can change directions at any moment.

In an unstructured environment, it is crucial for you to establish strict rules to guide your behavior. You can drown yourself with too many possibilities. Therefore, you will need to give yourself a direction and definition.

Since the market is unstructured, the game only begins when you decide to enter the market and ends only when you exit. You possess the freedom to structure the game any way you want. Given the unlimited potential for profit, entering the market will be easier than getting out.

Reasons Are Irrelevant

Some traders believe that if they can identify the reasons why the market performed the way it did, they can find out what the market will do next. This belief gives way to the assumption that the traders know their reasons too, and these will then help them in deciding their future.

The reasons traders would give are irrelevant. Most traders do not plan their trades, and that is why they do not know what they did and why. They act spontaneously and then add rationale to their behavior after the trade. These after-the-fact reasons are either justifications for what traders did or excuses for what they did not.

Risk/Reward Ratio

The risk/reward ratio tells a trader how much risk they are taking for exactly how much potential reward. It shows the potential rewards for each dollar a trader risks on an investment.

The calculation of this ratio is very easy. The maximum risk is divided by the net target profit. Decide where you want to enter the trade and choose where you would take your profit or your loss. When you have got your entry and exit targets, you can calculate the risk/reward ratio.

Calculating the risk/reward ratio of a trade is crucial as it helps a trader understand whether they should invest or not.

Risk Management

Cryptocurrency is not issued by a central authority. That makes it impervious to government interference and prone to risks.

Following are some examples of risks that endanger the growth of cryptocurrency in the market:

Cyber Risks

The security expertise is hardly keeping up with the growing demand for trading in cryptocurrencies. Businesses and individual investors are dealing with hackers that crash into crypto exchanges, clear out crypto wallets, and corrupt devices with malware that steal cryptocurrency. The traders also have to deal with complex ransomware, extortion events, etc. As deals are executed online, these hackers single out the people, servicing function and storage areas, making use of phishing and malware.

Furthermore, cryptocurrency highly relies on unregulated companies. Some of these may lack the needed internal constraints and therefore become more vulnerable to fraud and cyber-attacks than institutions that are regulated. Sourcing the blockchain technology to outside vendors might result in considerable third-party risk susceptibility.

Artificial intelligence-powered bots scour the Internet for weak links, increasing the risk of trading in cryptocurrency manifolds.

Operational Risks

The early adoption of cryptocurrencies was widely accepted because of their decentralized structure. They did not rely on the government and therefore had an ideological appeal. It was also popular in the countries where the government policies led to high inflation or very limited capital outflow. But with such decentralization, cryptocurrency transactions cannot be reversed in a coordinated manner. There is no pervasiveness, and it is obvious from the fact that Bitcoin is cryptographically protected. If you lose or forget your keys, you won't get access to your account.

The ledger is shared and operated by many nodes, but mining has become quite concentrated. The concentration of mining power leads to the concentration of voting power. This means that a union of a few largest miners can make the algorithm of the blockchain work in their favor. Thus, for a business building an application on a cryptocurrency blockchain, the concentration of mining power is fatal, as there lies the risk that a union of miners might change the underlying code.

Technological Risks

There are some technical limitations to cryptocurrencies. The computational complexity and energy expenditure of Bitcoin mining have been reported. This has probable risks to the asset class as well because of the general assertion that complex systems fail in complex ways. Not all cryptocurrencies are equally safe because the risk proofing provided by decentralized blockchain structures is not enjoyed by databases that are centralized.

Business Risks

As we know by now, cryptocurrencies are not backed by any organization of national or international acclaim, a central bank, or even any assets or other forms of credit. Their value is completely dependent on the traders that place value on them through their transactions. This means that loss of confidence can reduce trading activities in the market and an instantaneous drop in value.

There is also a significant risk to the reputation and brand of any financial institution involved in cryptocurrency-related activities. Their clients might not be elated about their divergence from conventional services and would refrain from investing in it as well.

Regulatory Risks

Bitcoin has a complex and decentralized nature. It also includes a considerable amount and variety of participants - senders, receivers, mining, trading platforms, etc. Thus, a single anti-money laundering (AML) approach does not exist.

There is a lack of coordination and clear regulations on the financial, legal, and other treatments of cryptocurrencies.

The fact that trading markets are brimming with risks is not unknown to man. There are inherent risks involved while dealing with cryptocurrencies as well, but there are methods to reduce them.

Here are a few steps to do just that and strengthen trust:

Regulatory Approval

The most effective way to reduce the inherent risk attached to cryptocurrency is by achieving regulatory approval, which is very ironic since the cryptocurrency has been popular because it is a decentralized currency without a regulatory framework whatsoever. This approval from a regulator would help build and improve the credibility of the currency and go a long way in reducing the risks associated with it.

The US dollar, the place of the reserve currency, would be the best point to start with - but not all US regulators are created equal. Cryptocurrency needs to cruise through the following five regulatory frameworks in order to gain traction in the United States:

Financial crimes-related regulations, like the Bank Secrecy Act (BSA), the USA Patriot Act, and the Office of Foreign Assets Control (OFAC)

State Banking Departments

The SEC

The Commodity Futures Trading Commission (CFTC), and

The Internal Revenue Service (FBAR, FACTA requirements).

The best result would be regulatory approval or agreements with all the given institutions, but that would be unlikely due to the vested interests of these bodies. A statement of approval from at least two of them would work to gain trust, which would help reduce risks.

Acceptance and/or Adoption by a Trusted Global Organization

As several institutions and companies invest in new technology, accepting and embracing a leading digital currency or at least supporting it can definitely make a difference.

Any financial institution taking on this venture would have to:

Educate their clients about prospective cryptocurrency risks and advantages

Portray an improved availability of its cryptocurrency offerings

Improve the reliability of cash exchanges, and

Offer an affordable level of protection to its clients.

Consumers would be more accepting if they will have access to innovative services that would be cost-effective as well as simple to use.

Implement Structural Mitigants

Reserve Requirements for Exchanges

Another way to reduce risk is to enhance the ecosystem so as to include more cryptocurrency exchanges. A cryptocurrency exchange operates as a broker and a custodian apart from an exchange. If these exchanges started the practice of holding a predetermined amount of reserves to survive any major downturn, adopting a few policies and practices as a clearinghouse, they would provide an extra amount of protection in times of market uncertainty as well as volatility.

Insurance Products

Insurance products offering investor protection, like FDIC insurance, could also help in the mitigation of risks involved in cryptocurrencies. A personal insurance policy could supplement such protection packages.

Take Advantage of Technology

Mobile phone technology has improved dramatically and has led to an increase in currency transferability.

Internet banking and other online payment methods, such as Apple Pay, Google Wallet, PayPal, etc., have increased consumer usage of mobile payment methods, and this has paved the way for the acceptance of cryptocurrency.

The growth and maturity of the cryptocurrency market might also lead to an increase in liquidity. This would considerably reduce exchange fees and price volatility. Merchants and other consumers that are opposed to risk will also experience reduced pressure to convert their cryptocurrency to fiat currency immediately.

Risk Management Framework

Effective risk documentation is extremely important. A standard risk management framework basically covers policies, methods, and standards relating to fraud, cyber risk, anti-money laundering, physical safety and security of assets, operational risk, IT security, etc. This management framework must be used at an institution-wide level as all the mentioned risks are related to each other. It will be more effective when business continuity and disaster recovery programs are added to the framework.

The risk framework also needs to be amplified by providing real-time information and scenario planning. Software upgrades also need to be given special attention. All participants involved in the cryptocurrency ecosystem should be risk assessed.

Financial Freedom While Trading in Cryptocurrency

With the rise of technology, every person is finding better ways to invest and expand their financial scores. A whole new generation of investors has welcomed various investment opportunities as a tool to achieve their financial freedom. Cryptocurrency markets are one such opportunity for these risk-takers. Crypto markets are not just another type of exchange like stocks and securities. They act as a key step in democratizing wealth.

Financial technology keeps charming the retail investors. Though sometimes, its cons outweigh its pros, which was seen recently in the first quarter of 2021. Investors got to witness the strength and problems of current financial markets.

Gamestop's huge appeal among retailers and investors on the WallStreetBets subreddit sent the stocks of the application soaring to $348 in the month of January, ultimately forcing the trading firms to close out short positions, costing them billions.

Trading apps that work with zero commission, such as Robinhood, experienced a large inflow of traders and retail investors, eventually forcing the platform to end trading GameStop for the short-term, forcing investors out of the market preventing them from investing further. The eventual criticism on various grounds by people called attention to the imbalance in economic power.

Cryptocurrencies such as Bitcoin and Ethereum have come out as a financial contraption over the last year. They have now gained new stature over the last quarter of the year, became financial fairness tools and platforms, and empowered traders and investors.

Since the last two years, various cryptocurrencies such as Monero, Dash, LiteCoin, and Bitcoin have become very popular among retail customers, changing the market share and reforming investor's interaction with financial institutions.

As per the verified report of Financial Conduct Authority's Cryptoasset Consumer Research Report 2020, around 77 percent of all the surveyed population bought crypto assets using an online exchange, and around 27 percent of them actually use crypto assets to buy goods and services. This report, therefore, clearly demonstrates how easy it is to buy cryptocurrency and use it as a commodity for exchange.

Continuing with the previous example, let us see how crypto has really changed the market situation. Applications such as Robinhood were created with the true objective of democratizing the investing process. However, they have clearly shown to the world that financial impartiality can only be achieved when all the parties have equal opportunity to use the same degree of control and knowledge.

Democratization has eventually opened the way for decentralization, a process where a single central authority is not brokering and controlling all the investors' actions. Instead of central authority, the traders and investors depend on blockchain technology to bargain directly with each other and make investments. The major benefit that decentralization provides is that it consigns the power back to its users. Cryptocurrencies such as Bitcoin were crafted as a decentralized and democratized substitute to traditional financial services and therefore did not have a single spot of weakness or failure, forcing them to be more efficient, popular, democratic, and resilient.

The cryptocurrency market acts as a strong tool in empowering its investors to take wealth building into their own hands by giving its agents access to wealth, without any moderator, where they can exchange on a virtual market with the assurance of security through blockchain. The trust of traders has been broken by the stock exchanges too many times, especially the financial crisis of 2008. This paved the way for cryptocurrencies and clearly provided an alternative view of how to build trust in the financial industry.

In the words of Charles Hoskinson, the co-founder of cryptocurrency Ethereum and current chief executive of crypto and blockchain company IOHK, "Our industry's technology is about brokering trust among people who don't trust each other."

As the future of investing is changing, so are its investors. There was a time when wealth was exclusive to high net worth individuals and financiers. But, Crypto markets have totally changed the scenario propelling the democratization and decentralization of wealth, eventually giving more financial freedom to the investors, and this is only the beginning.

Why Do Most Day Traders Lose?

Imagine three traders who placed the same trades, and all of them ended up losing money.

The first trader becomes disheartened, curses the market, and gives up for the day.

The second one gets frustrated, engages in revenge trading by trading more aggressively, and ends up losing even more by the end of the day.

The third trader pauses their trading, realigns their emotions, re-evaluates their strategy, waits for a clear opportunity, and places a good trade that ends up bringing her even by the end of the day.

How Are These Traders Different?

Success and failure in trading depend on the behavior and emotions of the traders.

An important reason why so many traders lose is that they take the losses and the downfalls in trading personally. They have an external locus of control. Their feelings, emotions, confidence, peace, etc., are connected to the trading results. They feel good when they do well and get frustrated, discouraged, doubtful of their abilities, etc.

Instead of developing the understanding that losses are a part of trading and dealing with their losses constructively, they personalize the trading events and react emotionally.

Successful traders trade for skill, and pretty much all professional traders conceal their profit/loss section during a trade. All they focus on is the execution of a profit target or a stop loss level. Traders who take every negative or positive trade they make as an opportunity to improve are the ones who consistently earn profits.

Some might find it surprising, but trading results can be affected by the level of alertness, energy, and overall health of the trader. Physical exhaustion, drowsiness, tension, etc., often affect your concentration level and eventually the decision process. You should try keeping a record of your physical state and trading results, and you will see how they affect each other.

It is tough to maintain a positive relationship between losses and your mental and emotional health. There are ways you must learn to make it easier for you to keep peace with losses in trading.

Trading can be extremely stressful. Active day trading is the most stressful of all. Do not make any trades if you are under pressure. You can be a good trader but a losing trader too.

Characteristics of Successful Traders

The personality traits of a trader are the unseen and intangible aspects of trading that are essential to support its more tangible facets.

Traders tend to spend more time on developing and grooming their technical knowledge of the market, but very little time and effort are put into growing and improving characteristics, such as their temperament, mindset, emotions, etc.

Many people might consider focus, passion, and determination to be the most important traits required to succeed in trading. These traits do have their strengths and can benefit the traders, but they aren't enough to sustain them. Traders must learn how to use their positions to their benefit and achieve returns, and control risk. Successful trading is a combination of technical and psychological skills. Thus, a great trader must have a combination of these skills and traits.

Some qualities and features that can make a trader successful are:

Practicing Discipline

Discipline is crucial if one wants to be successful in any job. Trading also requires a trader to be highly disciplined as all the hard work, effort, and preparation can be lost if there's a lack of discipline.

Disciplined traders are able to identify opportunities without losing precious time. They also do extensive research and plan their strategies and exit tactics well in advance. They do not lose focus of what they really want to achieve and make all the efforts they can into that direction.

Creating an independent trading strategy that is fit for you can help you practice discipline.

Learning from Losses

If you are on the route to becoming a trader, you need to be able to accept the fact that every trader loses money. What separates bad traders from successful ones is the ability to keep going despite the loss.

Although painful, incurring loss is a learning experience. You must take it as an opportunity to assess your strategy and adjust it for the better.

In order to develop this trait, a trader must start keeping a record of their actions and thoughts. Review and evaluate the way you behave. Always be open to receiving feedback. Monitor your growth on your own by making use of the mistakes you made in the past.

Being Consistent

If you wish to succeed at something, you must become consistent with it. Many traders focus unnecessary attention on their everyday profit and loss, and this leads them towards failure.

A smart trader must assess the trading situations and earn from them. You should not start giving back to the market only after a few big wins. Understanding positive months or years will enable you to speed up the process of achieving your goal. In this manner, you will learn to be consistent with trading.

Being Patient

If you are a beginner in the trading market, you should not anticipate that you would make huge profits right away. You need to invest your time, be patient and learn the ways of the market.

A successful trader will take losses expeditiously and will be slow to earn gains. Do not be in a hurry to take profits. Take your time to develop appropriate behaviors, practice them and create compatible ways to trade, and the profits will follow.

Traders must learn to be tolerant of the markets and trade only when they can fully exploit them.

Planning

Operating on instincts alone will not always work in your favor. Traders who plan in advance will probably have a better chance of winning.

Developing a logical plan and executing it is what experienced traders do. You will have no doubt about what you want and create ways to attain it if you decide to plan your moves before making them.

If a plan does not work for you, adjust it.

Respecting Uncertainty

Financial markets, as we all know, are complex systems. No one can see and understand the complete picture. Successful traders know this and respect the risk and uncertainty that come with trading. They accept the fact that no one can know what comes next.

There are a few behaviors that may be helpful in developing this trait. You must have a structured approach to trading and should also develop a strategic perspective. Always plan your trades and make sure that you include risk in trade evaluation. Develop an approach for the assessment of risk and reward.

Being Inquisitive

Successful traders know how to go through each trade and develop unique and better strategies every time. Losses do not perturb them. Instead, they analyze the trade and ask what could have been done differently to avoid this.

Inquisitiveness allows a trader to learn from their failures as well as others'.

Practicing Risk and Money Management

Successful traders treat trading as a business, so they know that it is stupid to enter into it without sufficient capital and liquidity. They are aware of the downfalls of not adhering to the basic principles of money management.

Simple acts, such as placing a huge trade, failing to assess the risk, and not having a proper exit strategy, can lead to losses.

Money management is the prosaic and unexciting aspect of trading, but it carries too much importance to be avoided just on account of being boring. It must be paid equal attention and treated as important as other key aspects of trading.

Maintaining Records

It is important to keep a track record of all your trades, as it will help you avoid making costly mistakes.

Keeping and maintaining a thorough record of trades is a sign of a sharp trader. This crucial habit provides them with all the information quickly so that they avoid past mistakes and save precious time.

Achieving Balance and Perspective in Life

Successful traders have a holistic perspective of life. They know that if trading is out of balance, it can affect other parts of their lives and vice-versa. This is why they will focus on other aspects of their life as much as they do on trading.

It is easy to forget that trading, too, has a human element to it. It is not limited to tools, electronic systems, and instruments. It is the human element that makes us successful.

Therefore, to become a successful trader, you must ensure that you make time for other interests and responsibilities. Develop objective thinking and practice ways to keep your mind clear. Focus on being fit and healthy, and do not take on extra work just to keep you busy.

Keep in mind that practice makes perfect. Be consistent with practicing these traits, and you will grow as a trader.

The Cycle of Emotions

When things go well, a trader feels like they have gained mastery over the game of investment. On the other hand, when things do not go in the expected direction, they get discouraged and move out of the game or engage in behaviors that lead to further losses.

As a beginner, it is important to understand that traders go through many emotions that vary in magnitude, given how good or bad the situation is. It is crucial to learn how either you or another trader might behave in response to the changing dynamics of trading.

The cycle of market emotions explains the relationship between a trader's feelings and judgments. Having an understanding of the role emotions play in the market cycle can help you avoid making decisions based on feelings. This will help you to tackle triggers that force you to buy and sell at the wrong time.

Stage 1: Optimism, Excitement, Thrill, and Euphoria

The cycle generally begins with optimism. Here, traders expect returns for the risk of investing. When things start moving in the expected direction, they get excited in anticipation of high returns.

Further, this excitement becomes thrilling as the market continues to be favorable. At this juncture, the traders have complete confidence in their trading system.

Euphoria is experienced at the top of the market cycle. This is the point of an extreme financial gamble but also equal gain. The investments bring quick profits, so the traders begin to ignore the important concept of risk.

Stage 2: Anxiety, Fear, Denial, and Desperation

When the markets first start to move in the opposite direction, traders become anxious. This anxiety turns into denial, and traders deny accepting that the market is going to fall.

Denial changes to fear when the investment value starts decreasing. At this point, the traders should try to get out with a small profit, but they do not, and all gains are lost. They become desperate and attempt to bring their positions back.

Stage 3: Panic, Capitulation, and Despondency

In this stage, the traders start to panic, as they are clueless and helpless. They feel like they have no control whatsoever and are completely at the mercy of the market.

To stop further losses, they sell their positions at any price available and leave the market.

The traders who still hold on experience despondency and wonder if they would ever recover or leave the market. However, the traders fail to recognize that they are at the rare position of maximum financial gains.

Stage 4: Depression, Hope, Respite, and Optimism

When losing, traders start questioning themselves about how they could have been so dumb.

When the markets start rising, they might become doubtful, thinking whether the market growth will last or not. When the rise continues, there is hope that they can still do this and realize that the market actually does have cycles.

The markets turn positive again, and there is a sense of relief. With every rise, the cycle moves towards faith and optimism.

Chapter Two: Getting Started

How Much Money Do You Need to Begin Day Trading?

Before deciding to invest in a trade, you should ask yourself if it is the perfect option for you and also how much you can spend. The answers depend on an accurate and genuine understanding of what the trade is all about. You need to consider the risks involved and must know how to control them.

Day trading can be profitable for those who are informed about the fundamentals of the trade. You do not need much money as long as it will help you to take home profit and cover fees. You can kick off this venture with just $10.

The minimum amount of money you can invest depends on the type of currency you choose to invest in and may differ in different exchanges. Other elements such as fees for trading such as marker and taker fees can also influence how much you end up paying. The spending is also dependent on the bid-ask spread and bank transfer fees. You must confirm your information about these factors with the platforms you are using for your trade.

Risks Involved in Day Trading

Here are some common risks associated with day trading and errors you must avoid:

Considerable amounts of time and effort are required. It is almost like getting a full-time job because it requires constant attention. You may end up losing your money if you do not put in the required effort.

There will be losses. Around 15% of traders are successful in their first strike. Even as an expert, there will be losses from time to time.

Trading is very close to gambling, and you might get addicted to it. When you wonder about the potential of earning huge amounts of money with just a click, it can be emotionally engrossing. If left uncontrolled, this habit might be destructive.

Day trading is risky. You must avoid investing more than you can afford to lose.

Choosing Which Cryptocurrencies to Trade

With a little bit of research, choosing a cryptocurrency to invest in can be an easy task. It is all about the fundamentals.

The Community

A huge part of a digital currency's success is its following. You must think about investing in cryptocurrencies that have a strong community and a significant amount of loyal and trustworthy followers. This would be a reflection of the fact that people have an actual interest and faith in that cryptocurrency.

Go through some Reddits, check out some channels and blogs on YouTube, crosscheck some feedback from their communities, and look out for what they have to say about your future investment in the currency.

If you have confusion regarding coins, looking out for a few forums and researching the community on Reddit is a great methodology for getting to know and comprehending the hysteria behind an altcoin. This way you can really know if you should invest in it.

In addition to judging the popularity of a cryptocurrency, the community can also be helpful in making you understand some of the more difficult and technical jargon of the trading world by breaking it down into simpler terms.

Bigger cryptocurrency communities generally have operative and functional Reddit communities and other forums, but the smaller communities are also very obliging and eager to help, as this is the way they will also be able to become a larger community.

Fundamental Analysis

In simple terms, fundamental analysis refers to the foundation of an investment - their ambitions and goals, their team, their strengths, and other qualities, etc. If you want to be in the trading environment for a long time, you must pay equal attention to fundamental and technical analysis. They are both very detrimental to your success if you are in it for the long haul.

Most people in the market are running after low-quality altcoins, and fundamental analysis helps you to avoid making this mistake by separating the good from the bad.

Grasping the knowledge of how to go about fundamental analysis will assist you in making better choices regarding investment in cryptocurrencies. Here are some methods you could follow:

Research the Team

The most important thing to research before investing is the team behind a cryptocurrency.

You must analyze the following points:

Who is responsible for the cryptocurrency?

Do you have faith in their ability and expertise?

Do they have ambition?

Do they have a strong history of success?

All of these questions are crucial to consider when choosing a cryptocurrency, as the answers can lead them to a favorable outcome or failure.

The Technology

The underlying technology is an extremely important part of a cryptocurrency's success. You must analyze and understand how the technology is different from other cryptocurrencies and how it is going to perform against its competitors. Ethereum could be taken as an example of a cryptocurrency doing great in the context of technology because of the following:

Smart contracts - Technology that provides a platform for the exchange of everything that has value.

The technology used in Ethereum is created really well. It makes it straightforward for developers to connect the blockchain with the applications they own.

Ethereum Virtual Machine Technology (EVM) - This technology provides developers easy ways to design and develop applications on a larger scale.

Because of its innovative technology, Ethereum has become a huge cryptocurrency.

The White Paper

When a new cryptocurrency is released, a white paper is published as well. The paper provides a brief description of the coin, the technology involved, how it works, and its overall vision.

Reading the white paper is the ultimate step you can take to start your fundamental analysis of the coin. You must not invest your capital into the currency until you have gone through their white paper.

There are technical terms included in the description but do not let that stop you from evaluating the white paper. It can provide a rich source of knowledge about the currency, and that is why it is definitely worth reading. A white paper can also be used to know about the cryptocurrency's professionalism and credibility. Here are some red flags to watch out for when investing in a cryptocurrency:

Is the currency you are investing in making any unrealistic promises?

Is the white paper ambitious in context with its objectives?

The Cryptocurrency's Vision

Before investing, you do want to ensure that this coin is here to stay and will be around for a minimum of 5-10 years. A big vision represents a great objective, and if they are not thinking long term, then you must reconsider your investment.

The coin will face serious struggles in order to find a place among the competitors if it does not have a clear vision and a mission.

Always try to recognize their intentions regarding the future of the coin, whether you are going through their social media, their website, or reading their white paper.

Also, look at the type of culture being created in the community.

You must always invest your time and capital in a cryptocurrency, which has a solid vision. Ensure that it can be persistent and be effective in the long run. Although short-term profits can be rousing, and you may be thinking about swing trading, you must continue to focus on the vision and reflect upon the question of where this currency is going to be in the coming 10-20 years.

Their Leadership

The leadership team of a cryptocurrency is exceedingly important, as they are the ones responsible for making all the important decisions. The leaders carry out the vision of the currency. Therefore, it is vital that you analyze their team and take a look at their achievements so far.

You want to be satisfied with their expertise. You should also make sure that they are the champions of the vision and that they possess the ability to lead their coin to success.

Do check if they are personally invested in the project.

Look at their experience and check out the other cryptocurrency-related projects they have handled.

What is their reputation as a CEO?

Pricing History

The pricing fluctuations provide you with a strong background of the coin, and you can judge if it will be worthwhile to invest in it for the future.

You must check:

Are they liable to change rapidly? Experience unpredictability oftentimes?

Was the coin resilient when the market went down?

Are they experiencing a record high in their prices?

If the coin has been priced at an all-time high, it is advisable to wait until the value of the cryptocurrency drops.

Some people want to try to predict the price movements of a currency by analyzing its pricing history. It is a matter of chance. Nobody is going to be correct with the forecast every time.

Credibility and Reputation

You must check out if the cryptocurrency is respected online and if they have a robust reputation.

A currency needs to be credible and trustworthy for you to be convinced of making an investment in them. If they have amassed a reputation for being untrustworthy, then you know that you should not invest your capital into them.

So make a few Google searches, navigate your search through crypto communities and find out what people are saying about the coin. You want to invest in a coin that people feel positive about. This way, you can avoid scams.

The Road Map

When you're looking for a cryptocurrency to invest in, you should look for a coin that has strong plans for continuous development, a coin with a solid road map.

There must be clear and precise timelines for the development of the coin. Lack of a proper timeline could reflect the absence of commitment in the team.

When are major updates being released? What is the plan?

There are definitely no "safe bets" in the cryptocurrency world. However, these points will really prove helpful to you in picking out a strong investment or at least eliminating non-deserving investments.

Before making a decision and choosing a cryptocurrency to invest in, go through this guide and make sure your potential future investment has all the needed qualities.

Market Cycles

A market cycle is a pattern or trend that appears at different times. Generally speaking, market cycles on higher time frames have more reliability than market cycles on lower time frames.

While asset values might give the impression of moving aimlessly up and down, technical analysis indicates specific repetitive cycles. These are mainly steered by the market shifts brought about by big investors.

It is noteworthy that it is almost impossible to know at any given moment where we currently are in a market cycle. This can only be determined after that part of the cycle has concluded.

Market cycles include the following phases:

Expansion/Accumulation

This phase of the market cycle transpires as a consequence of economic growth. It leads to a bull market when traders attempt to buy. In a well-managed economy, expansion can continue for a long time.

Peak/Markup

The pressure to buy reaches its peak and transitions to the next stage as large investors are no longer interested in buying overpriced assets.

Contraction/Distribution

This stage of the market cycle shows the decline of the market. Economists consider this period as a market recession.

Trough/Markdown

The market has reached its lowest point by this phase and begins to move to the expansion phase.

Drivers of Market Cycles

Although there are many explanations for the occurrence of market cycles, the main are macroeconomic components - inflation, economic growth rates, interest rates, and rate of unemployment.

Interest rates are anticipated to stimulate economic growth. Therefore, they will generally send markets higher. Additionally, an increase in inflation is a typical signal of an imminent surge in interest rates, and this causes constriction of the market and slows down economic growth. A rise in the levels of unemployment also is an indicator of economic slowdown.

The market sentiment also decides the direction of market cycles. Due to several circumstances, there may be a boom period where traders hurry to buy certain assets as well as periods where investors sell in substantial amounts because of the panic in the market.

Day Trading vs. Swing Trading

Things Investors Need to Know

During trading in cryptocurrency, the timing can remarkably impact our strategy and eventual profitability. Day traders open and close several positions in a single day, whereas swing traders take trades that continue for two or more days, weeks, and sometimes even months. The two given trading styles suit differently to different traders, considering certain factors such as availability of time, psychology of the trader, market atmosphere, and most crucially - the amount of capital available.

Choosing between day trading and swing trading is not an easy task in itself. Let's discuss how each kind of trading works and what it requires from the beginning until the end.

How Does Day Trading Work?

The term 'day trading' arises from the idea that traders trade (buy and sell) their business in a day, often several times a day. People who invest in day trading look for rapid results in compounding returns. In the community of day traders, the "1% risk rule" is commonly followed. It guides a trader and says they must never risk beyond 1% of his portfolio on any particular trade.

Let's understand this with the help of an example. Suppose a trader risks 1% of their investment on each trade. If they experience loss by chance, they will lose 1%, but if they win, they will make 2% (2:1- reward to risk ratio). Let's suppose they manage to secure half of their trades. If this trader makes six trades a day on average, they will be adding 3% to their account balance every day, minus the trading fees. So, if the trader makes 2% a day, it would be about 200% over the year, uncompounded.

On the other side, though the numbers appear to be simple enough to change into big returns, nothing is ever really easy. Gaining almost twice the amount on winning trades as much as you lost on losers does not come without any challenges. You can possibly make swift profits, but you are also liable to exhaust your trading account in day trading quickly.

How Does Swing Trading Work?

Unlike day trading that usually involves more than one trade every day, swing trading is a process of trading over a few days, months, or perhaps, a few months. This results in the accumulation of losses and gains more slowly in comparison to day trades. However, there are always some particular swing trades that lead to huge profits or losses. Let's understand this with an example.

Assume a certain trader practicing swing trading uses the one particular risk management rule and risks 50% of their total investment on each trade to try to get 2-4% on the trades they are winning. Now assume that, on average, they earn 3% on winning trades and lose 1.5% on trades they lose on. They conduct six trades every month, of which 50% result in loss and 50% in win. A swing trader can earn 4.5% on the balance in their account, indicating less or fewer fees, in a month. That total amounts to around 36% in the year, which, although it appears great, provides less potential than a day trader's conceivable profits.

Time Spent in Trading

Day trading and swing trading need a lot of time, but typically day trading requires and uses more time than the latter.

Day Trading

Day traders spend no less than two hours each day in trading. If we add the time needed to prepare and chart/ trading review, it means spending four to five hours each day on your computer. If this trader decides to make more trades per day, his screen time considerably increases, and day trading could seem like any other time-taking career. Also, time investment adds to the pragmatic knowledge and experience of the trader, making him more efficient and confident.

Swing Trading

If we draw a comparison between the two, swing trading considerably consumes less time than day trading. For instance, if a trader is swing trading on a daily chart, he could discover new trades and also revise orders on ongoing positions in about 45 to 50 minutes per night. Sometimes, this activity does not even need to be done every night.

Traders involved in swing trading who take trades that go on for weeks or even months might only have to conduct trades and update their orders on a weekly basis, reducing the time given by the swing trader from an hour per day to an hour each week.

How to Choose Between Swing Trading and Day Trading

Both need a great deal of effort, efficiency, and expertise to produce consistent profits over a long time. 'Knowledge' here doesn't refer to bookish smartness. Success in trading is an outcome of attempting to find a strategy that cuts losses and produces profit over a considerable amount of trades, and then implementing that same strategy effectively with required flexibility time and again. Steady results are earned when a certain strategy is executed under countless variable situations in the market. This is a time-consuming process, and one should make several trades in a demo account to learn and gain experience before investing significant amounts of capital.

Swing and day traders share the same goal – making money. What differs is their styles, ways of working, and expected level of expertise at trading.

If a person is willing to invest in understanding the technical analysis tools and use them to his best advantage for major profits, they can become a swing trader. However, they must excel at using these tools to their advantage. Day traders, too, need to be really good with software and charting systems as they will be using them more often than swing traders.

Experts are divided between which trading offers more benefit. Some side with day trading, whereas others stand with swing trading since its wider timing window offers more potential for higher profits.

This does not mean that swing trading does not have its share of related risks. It can be stressful too. But if a trader is just a beginner, it could be contemplated as a safer option for the trader.

Another important aspect to consider is day trading usually involves working with margin, i.e., borrowed capital. Trading on borrowed capital has its own pros and cons. On the one hand, it enables day traders to maximize their profits. On the other, it can also land them in red rapidly if the execution of the strategies goes wrong or strategies themselves were faulty in the first place. Compared to this, swing trading can be quoted as less risky, but the risk does not vanish completely, and the trader needs to be careful all the time.

Points to ponder before making the decision:

Pace

As already learned, the pace of day trading is very rapid, whereas, in swing trading, trades can carry on for days, weeks, or months. Depending upon your caliber, pick your pace and lead with it.

Stress

Day trading entails more tension, as one has to keep eyes on the trades for at least 2 hours every day on a daily basis. In swing trading, traders have to update their trades once in 2-3 days or maybe only on a weekly basis. Stress can confuse and consume you leading you to losses.

Freedom

One can very much argue that swing traders have comparably more freedom than day traders since their trading process is spread over a longer period.

Focus

Due to the fast rate, brief trade process, and window opportunity, day trading needs strengthened emphasis for an extended period. Swing trading also expects focus, but there are much lengthier gaps between activities such as entering and exiting trades. So, day trades require a more focused approach than swing trades.

Beginners are much better off with swing trading than day trading. The latter puts you in direct competition with major investors and traders who use cutting-edge technology and software to always stay at the top of their game and retain huge profits. Swing trading requires less and cheap resources. A basic computer and free software would do the required work. There are thousands of free resources available to choose from to maximize advantage, but you need to tread carefully.

When comparing day trading and swing trading, you should ask certain questions necessary to reach a satisfactory answer.

Can you give a full commitment?

Can you make fast decisions?

What is more important - relaxation or work?

Are you a risk-taker?

Can you work under pressure?

When Should You Choose Swing Trade?

If the given description agrees with your way of working, the swing trading option might prove to be a better person for you.

You are ready to wait from a few days, weeks to months to study the market system and its movements.

You are already financially stable or getting into trading as a spare job and not a full-time job.

Constant monitoring the market movements is not your cup of tea. Babysitting the system to read fluctuations requires a lot of time.

You want a lesser stressful option that does not get in the way of your relaxation.

Trading is not the only thing you want to rely on for your financial needs.

You do not have a huge amount of capital available all the time.

You do not have any or advanced levels of technical trading knowledge.

When Should You Choose Day Trade?

You have a huge amount of capital required under the rules.

You can make decisions at a quick pace, and you have time to study up-to-the-minute trends.

Pressure does not affect the quality of your work, and you can manage your stress and do not stress over small things.

You understand the associated risks, making major losses and ending up in debt.

You are okay with small profits also. Not winning a big game will not affect you deeply.

Tools and Platforms

The cryptocurrency market is filled with risks and fluctuations. There are people who consistently gain profits, and there are others who invariably lose. There are many deciding factors that lead to losses and gains, such as technology available, type of trading, working capital, experience, etc.

One such important deciding factor that separates winners from losers is crypto tools and platforms. Thousands of such tools can be obtained from the market, but it is up to the trader to choose the best ones.

Networking with different people in the crypto industry should be an incessant task, but there is always a factor of luck in meeting the ideal investors.

It can be the variation between finding out the next hidden gem that can enhance your portfolio or follow the crowd and buy the overpriced cryptocurrencies.

Let us check some of the most promising crypto tools and platforms that make them available easily to the trader. These tools can entirely modify the way investors interact in the crypto atmosphere.

Best Exchanges

The initial step in profiting big in the crypto market is choosing the dependable and authentic exchanges to use. They are the investor's doors to the crypto community. Factors through which one can differentiate between useful exchange and useless exchange are security, liquidity, and fees are given below:

Security is a crucial part of selecting a legitimate exchange. By holding money on the exchange, you essentially trust them with its safekeeping. So, their security must ensure optimum protection. Exchanges are always under attack from hackers. For example, hackers siphoned millions of funds from a market exchange named Cryptopia in 2019. Although these funds have been reimbursed to investors, the whole exchange would have come crashing down if the hackers could not have been tracked.

How quickly and easily assets can be purchased and sold is known as its liquidity.

The higher the liquidity, the better the market exchange is. If the market is quite liquid, it is almost certain there will be a buyer or a seller to fulfill your order request at all times.

The next factor you need to pay attention to are the fees payable. Top traders in the market are always aware of the fees, usually because they have a margin of profit in it. So it is recommended to find market exchanges that are not reliable and liquid but also cheap.

Some of the best exchanges are:

Binance

Speaking in terms of trading volume, Binance occupies a leading position. This platform boasts of high liquidity and transactions. It is also an industry leader in terms of the number of registered users it has. It has a clean track record, a trustworthy team, and high quality of security.

BitMex

This market exchange offers up to 100 times leverage, which signifies a high-risk, high reward. It is based in Hong Kong, and its security has never been jeopardized. It is a high-quality platform for risk-taking traders.

Best Decentralized Exchange

The only difference between a decentralized and a centralized exchange is their technical infrastructure. The primary advantage of selecting a decentralized exchange is the users don't have the deposit their funds with the exchange. Instead, their capital can be stored within virtual wallets. Although users benefit from greater security at

DEXs, less liquidity and difficulty in its usage lessen their appeal to the traders.

IDEX

One of the earliest decentralized exchanges that are still in the race today is IDEX. This exchange is web-based, and it has an elegant user interface. Their liquidity level is also reliable, so an average trader does not face any issues in getting the orders filled.

Trading Platforms

Trading platforms are among the most important crypto tools, and they can considerably improve your game plan by streamlining it. You don't need to open multiple windows for trading on different exchanges. Instead, you can do it all from a single platform. It means you get a chance to make the most of the opportunities that present themselves while closely monitoring the market and its general sentiments. Coinigy and Tradedash are among the best trading platforms available these days.

Coinigy

It is one of the most popular and widely used platforms these days. It was launched in 2014 and is steadily growing since then. It supports more than 45 exchanges, a variety of trading charts and offers excellent support. If you are interested in developing your own trading strategies, don't forget to explore their paid option of purchasing historical data.

Tradedash

Tradedash supports Bittrex and Binance. By using this platform, you have easy access to two of the biggest exchanges available in the market. Their massive user base increases the liquidity. Tradedash is a desktop-based application, unlike web-based Coinigy. All the keys to access the platform are encrypted and stocked on your personal desktop. This further strengthens the security offered by this platform.

Charting Tools

This wonderful tool lets users draw trend lines based on trading indicators to understand how the market might be functioning. When you start practicing with such trade lines, you can effectively hone your skills and obtain the required experience to understand technical analysis thoroughly. If you become a pro at technical analysis, it becomes easier for you to win big.

Some of the best charting tools are:

TradingView

Make the most of its live trading charts available for cryptos and stocks alike on this platform. It offers a massive range of technical indicators and is considered to be one of the biggest providers of charting services. When it comes to exploring the functionalities offered by this platform, users can choose from premium and free versions.

Cryptowatch

Kraken, one of the most popular and massive crypto exchanges, owns Cryptowatch. It is a free tool and offers a variety of benefits. You can use it to chart markets across different coins. It also gives you a chance to view over ten charts in one go.

Market Data

This platform offers accurate real-time information about the total supply in the market, the circulating supply, and even information about price action. If you want to become a successful investor, you need to have a thorough understanding of the pulse of the market. The greater your accuracy, the better your chances of making informed trades.

Best places to find Market Data are:

Don't Miss a Hard Fork, Block Halving, or Swap

Never solely rely on news articles for gathering the information needed to trade in cryptocurrencies. Instead, you need to rely on calendar services to plan ahead. All the information available on this platform is compiled by experts and offers a quick view of all upcoming events.

Some of the Calendar Tools are:

CoinMarketCal

CoinMarketCal offers access to the latest and most comprehensive news about anything and everything associated with cryptos. The more information you have, the higher are the chances of making sound trades. It also shows information about any upcoming coin events. Here, we can search for our own coin too.

Coindar

It is quite similar to the tool mentioned above. Its easy-to-use interface makes it beginner-friendly. It also offers news about any major events or happenings associated with crypto at a glance.

Network Statistics

You should always be aware of everything that's happening in your surroundings. The same rule is applicable if you want to start trading in cryptocurrencies. These days, information is available at the click of a button. Unfortunately, there are thousands of fake articles circulating online too. From fake articles about the downfall of Bitcoin transactions to extremely high fees, there are several things you need to watch out for. All traders, especially beginners, should see for themselves how active the network of Bitcoin actually is. They should also see the active involvement of the development team so they can make their own decisions.

Most of the transactional activity that takes place on the cryptocurrency network shows price movements in the future. If an investor can efficiently read these activities and make rapid decisions after doing substantial research, it will certainly give him an advantage over others.

To gather some insights about network activities, one can use:

BitcoinVisuals

This tool will help regarding information related to Bitcoin only.

The hash rate is essentially the median fee applicable but transaction. By using this, you can realize how well the network is doing, at least from a technical perspective. For instance, if applicable fees have been reduced while the number of miners is increasing, it means the network is quite safe. It is also a sign that more and more people are interested in this. You can use this knowledge to your advantage and gain an edge over others in the market. Also, this platform helps to segregate fake news and real news. If you see news articles making claims that a certain cryptocurrency is dying, you can check the facts for yourself on this platform.

CryptoMiso

This platform, unlike BitcoinVisuals, is for all sorts of coins, not just Bitcoin. It is crucial to ensure that open-sourced projects are active when analyzing a coin. A simple assumption that you need to function on is associated with the level of activity. It is a dead-end if there is no activity. All this information can be easily verified on CryptoMiso.

Block Explorers

Block explorer essentially refers to a specific user interface you can use to interact with different blockchains. By doing this, you can easily view the transactional data available on the network. From seeing whether a cryptocurrency is sent or received to confirm the number of transactions on the network, there is a lot you can do. You can also use block explorers for the following.

Transaction sizes

Current block height

Largest wallets

Number of coin holders

Number of outstanding transactions

Number of past transactions on the network

Few great Blockchain Explorers are:

Coinmarketcap.com

For searching a coin on Coinmarketcap.com 0, click on " Explorer" to the left. If a specific crypto you are looking for isn't listed here, you can find it within the block explorer from their website. Alternatively, try searching for the coin name combined with the block explorer on Google.

Shrimpy

Unlike 3Commas, Shrimpy is a free rebalancer and backtester. It not only gives you a chance to re-balance portfolios but allows you to test different trading strategies through their backtesting feature available for the exchanges supported by this platform. Trades worth over $250,000,000 were executed on this platform.

Portfolio Trackers

If you want to keep a check on the pulse of your portfolio, you should use a portfolio tracker. It essentially lets you check the total value of all the investments while viewing the performance of each cryptocurrency. You can also use these platforms for checking any change in the value of your portfolio within every 24-hours.

After assessing your coins, you can make an informed decision of exchanging the loss-inducing coins. Some amazing portfolio trackers are:

Blockfolio

It is available only for mobile phones. It has the largest user base in the market. Blockfolio has a smooth user interface. It also includes a news section and signals in it. Having to enter your coins manually might seem like a disadvantage to some, but it seems like a significant advantage from a security perspective.

Blox

It comes in two versions - free and premium. Blox is a perfect portfolio tracker for traders who need a professional web-based solution for their business.

Cointracking

This is an affordable option. Its cheap cost does not mean cheap quality. Cointracking is associated with almost all the market exchanges. This tool calculates all the historical data of its users automatically upon importing their trades.

CoinStats

As with Blockfolio, even CoinStats is a mobile-only application. That said, you could use it for importing all your trades using its Application Programming Interface. You can save a lot of time by opting for this extremely convenient option.

Cointracking.info

It allows its users to import all their historical transaction data either through API or manually.

Unless you are prepared to take on a hands-on approach, you cannot test the different strategies or the tools discussed in the section. Start by trying the free tools, develop skills and experience, make them a part of your routine and finally throw yourself in the fire. A lot of investors do not even know about these tools, so you already have the edge over them. Keep trying these tools and keep making your own strategies and keep improving them. See what works the best for you, and move forward.

Chapter Three: Introduction to Technical Analysis

Technical Analysis

Understanding and analyzing the past price action, trading volume and charts, and using indicators to predict future price movement is known as technical analysis. The primary idea is to use past price action so the trader can understand how the market might behave in the future. Whether you are looking at daily, weekly, monthly, or yearly data, technical analysis works for all timeframes equally well. It is also applicable to different markets where the forces of demand and supply govern the price of instruments. Barring the acts of God, technical analysis takes into account everything that can impact the prices. Technical analysis can be used to understand risk management. It offers a solid model to analyze the market structure and obtain better insights into heart functions.

The practice of technical analysis is widely used among cryptocurrency traders because the valuation of cryptocurrency markets is largely based on speculation that can be handled only through technical factors.

Bases of Technical Analysis

Price Discounts Everything

Technical analysis removes the need to consider the company's fundamental and other economic factors separately.

It assumes that market psychology and all the other elements associated with it are included in the price of the stock. So, this analysis essentially helps determine and analyze the price movement because it is once again based on the force of demand and supply existing in the market.

The basic idea behind technical analysis is to trade with the trend. Whenever a trend moves in the market, you can expect its future price to move in the same direction as the trend was moving. For instance, if the trend suggests there's an upward price movement, a basic assumption is to believe the price will keep moving in this direction instead of against it.

History Repeats Itself

Traders have used charts and patterns for several decades. They can be used to identify any patterns associated with price movements. It usually so happens that trends tend to repeat themselves. Market psychology is believed to be the primary reason responsible for such recurring price movements.

Basics of Technical Analysis

Long Position

Whenever a trader purchases an asset because he believes its value will increase with time, it is a long position. This is one of the most common ways in which beginners start investing in financial products. You are essentially going long for an extended time whenever you select a long-term trading strategy such as buy and hold. It assumes that the value of the underlying asset will increase with time.

Short Position

This brings us to another common trading strategy which is holding a short position. In this, the trader is essentially selling his assets because he wants to repurchase them at a lower price later. This shares certain similarities with margin trading because you are essentially trading with borrowed assets. It is also known as shorting. This technique is commonly used in the derivatives market.

Order Book

When all currently open orders for assets are salted according to that price, it's known as an order book. Whenever an order is posted and not promptly felt, it will be added to the order book. It stays there until the order is either fulfilled or is canceled. When it comes to trading cryptocurrency on exchanges, a system known as a matching engine exists - in this system, the orders in the matching engine must match the ones mentioned in the order book. This entire mechanism is responsible for the execution of various trades on crypto exchanges. Order Books and this system is key to the concept of electronic exchange.

Order Book Depth

The order book depth or market depth is the display of the orders that are currently open in the order book. All the buy and sell orders are displayed cumulatively on a chart, making it easier for traders to understand what they're doing. The depth of the order book essentially refers to the liquidity that an order book can absorb. A market with high liquidity can absorb bigger orders without such orders affecting the price. On the other hand, large orders tend to significantly affect the price when the market is not liquid.

Market Order

Whenever an order is placed for buying or selling at the existing market price, it is known as a market order. This is perhaps the quickest way to enter and exit a market. Large traders or whales usually exert significant influence on the existing price within the market whenever they place market orders. The market order keeps fulfilling orders present in the order book until the entire order is fulfilled.

Limit Order

Whenever an asset needs to be purchased or sold at a specific price, it is known as a limit order. It was also known as the price limit. Limit sell orders are usually executed at either the limit price or a price that is higher than it. On the other hand, limit-by orders are usually executed at the limit price or a price lower than at. Whenever a trader wants to have better control over their entry and exit points in the market, they should use limit orders. One disadvantage of using such orders is the market might never reach the desired price. In such cases, the order is never fulfilled. This way, you can lose a trade opportunity with a potential for profit.

Stop-Loss Order

These types of orders only become active when a specific price level is reached. It is also known as a stop price.

The main purpose of this order is to limit losses. Every trade needs to define the price level in advance. It is called an invalidation point. This is the point where a trader must leave the market to prevent consequent losses. So, the invalidation point is the point where a trader would usually put the stop-loss order.

The stop-loss order can be a limit order as well as a market order. Whenever the market reaches the stop price, either a limit or the market order itself is activated.

Bid-Ask Spread

The bid is the highest buy order, while ask is the lowest sell order. The difference between the highest bid and the lowest ask is known as the bid-ask spread, and you can use this spread for measuring the liquidity present within a market. If this spread is quite small, it means the market is extremely liquid. The smaller the spread, the higher the liquidity. You can also use it to measure the existing supply and demand for a specific asset. The ask side is representative of the supply, and the bid side shows the demand.

Price Action and Mass Psychology

Traders can be divided into:

Buyers

Sellers, and the

Undecided

In any given market, buyers will try to reduce the buying price as much as they possibly can, while sellers will look forward to selling at the highest price. The amount a specific seller asks for his stock is known as the ask. The price at which a buyer offers to purchase a position is the bid. The actual prices would be decided by the actions of all traders in the market at any given moment regardless of whether they are buyers, sellers, or still undecided.

The pressure increases for bears and bulls due to the undecided players in the market. By now, you understand how the forces of demand and supply work. All the actions of sellers and buyers cost price fluctuations. Unfortunately, when the bears and bulls are aware of the fact that they are surrounded by several undecided traders who can stop in at any given point and turn the tide against them. If buyers take too much time to decide on a transaction, someone else could beat them in this race and eventually drive up the price. Similarly, sellers also know if they keep holding out expecting higher prices, some other seller might swoop in with a lower ask and reduce the current price in the market. It is usually the presence of the undecided traders that makes the buyers and sellers more than willing to deal with their opponents.

The buyers expect that the prices will go up, and that forces them to buy.

Whenever the bulls engage in buying, the market moves upward. It essentially means the buyers don't mind spending higher and higher prices to make the purchases. They are effectively bidding on top of each other. They do this because they are worried about missing out on a brilliant opportunity if they don't make the purchase right away. Doe price increases expedited by undecided traders who create a sense of urgency among the buyers. When the buyers start buying as soon as possible, the underlying security price will automatically increase.

On the other hand, sellers start selling because of their inherent expectation that the price will reduce. The market moves downward when the bears start selling. It means the sellers sell for lower and lower prices for positions they are holding because they are worried they might not get a chance to sell it for a better price. Eventually, they end up selling at prices that are quite low because they don't want to miss out on the opportunity. Once again, undecided traders have the power of pushing the prices down further by creating a sense of urgency among the sellers.

A trader will become successful if he can determine who will control the market and make his trades accordingly. All traders must carefully analyze the market and study the historical data to make calculated bets. They should also learn to make the most of the power between sellers and buyers while betting on a group they think will win.

Fortunately enough, candlestick charts showcase the general psychology of the market in action. The price action is a representation of how the traders are performing or feeling at any given point.

Candlesticks

Candlestick patterns provide Traders helpful information about the overall trend of a specific stock and the power wielded by buyers and sellers in a given market. Candlesticks are believed to be born neutral. They either become bearish or bullish depending on other circumstances. On certain rare occasions, they still maintain their neutrality. Traders are usually unaware of what candlesticks mean. Whenever a candle presents itself in the market, a battle ensues between bears and bulls. The winner will be reflected by the candle. If the buyers are regulating the price, the candle tends to move and becomes bullish while it becomes bearish once sellers are in control.

There are several other representations for price action in the market other than Candlestick charting. You can use numbers and figures, lines and points, and bars as well. Candlestick charts are visually appealing and easier to analyze and interpret than any other means. Every candlestick is nothing but a representation of its underlying price action. When you understand the different types of candles come it becomes easier to understand how the market is functioning at any given point.

Bearish Candlesticks

As the name suggests, they have bearish bodies. Such candlesticks show a market where the sellers are regulating the price action. It essentially means now is not the right time to buy anything in the market. If the market begins and ends at a high and low, the bearish candlesticks are filled or big-bodied. This essentially signals the market has a bearish tendency. By learning to read and interpret candlesticks, you will have a rough idea of the general attitude prevalent in the market. This is known as price action. It determines who is regulating the price in the market. Understanding the general attitude in the market makes it easier to determine when you should buy or sell. For instance, buy and hold securities if the bulls have a stronghold. Similarly, sell and short-sell if bears are ruling the market. Understanding price action is an important skill for all traders, especially day traders. If you don't want to be caught on the wrong side of a trade, learn to read candlesticks. All wise and experienced traders don't just jump into a position. Instead, they read the market and open or close a position only after they are certain of which way the wind is blowing.

Indecision Candlesticks

Spinning Tops

Any candle with high and low wicks of the same size and a larger than usual body are known as spinning tops. They are also known as indecision candles because it shows an indecisive state of the market. It essentially suggests the power wielded by buyers and sellers is the same in the market or almost equal. No one is singularly influencing the price, and this fight will keep going. With these candlesticks, the volume is low. A seasoned trader in such instances would wait and let the fight unfold between buyers and sellers before taking a position.

Dojis: Simple, Shooting Star, Hammer

Dojis is an important pattern of candlesticks, and they come in a variety of shapes and sizes. They generally don't have a body or have an extremely small body. They share certain similarities with a spinning top and are also known as indecision candlesticks. If there's a doji present on the chart, it means a fight is brewing between bulls and bears, and there isn't a clear winner.

If the high and low wicks of the dojis are similarly sized, they are known as simple dojis. At times, their top and bottom wicks are of varying lengths too. When the buyers are trying to push the price higher in the market but aren't successful, the top wick is usually longer. Such dojis are also indecision candlesticks but indicate that the sellers in the market will soon regain control.

In hammer Dojis, the lower wick is usually longer. This essentially means the sellers in the market tried to create a downward price trend but weren't successful. This can be interpreted as a likely takeover by the bulls in the market. Regardless of the shape of the Doji, it represents indecision prevalent in the market. If the bulls have exhausted their resources and the bears are trying to gain control of the market price, a bullish trend will form in the Doji. On the other hand, a bearish trend occurs when the sellers have exhausted their resources and the control reverts to the bulls fighting for price control.

All shapes of Dojis indicate indecision and possible reversals if they form a trend. If a Doji forms a bullish trend, it indicates that the bulls have become exhausted and that the bears are fighting to gain control of the price. In the same manner, if a Doji forms a bearish trend, it suggests that the bears (sellers) have become exhausted and that the bulls (buyers) are fighting back to take control of the price.

Learning to recognize these candlesticks is an important skill. However, it isn't the only skill you will need to become a successful trader. Understand that candles are by no means perfect. Don't make the mistake of placing trades whenever you notice the formation of a Doji. Always opt for a combination of analytical tools and techniques to determine the market's pattern.

Before using candlesticks, it is important to determine they simply represent a sense of indecision prevalent in the market and don't guarantee a reversal.

Candlestick Patterns

Bullish Patterns

These patterns may indicate a reversal of price movement. They are a signal for traders to consider opening a long position to profit from any upward course.

Hammer

This pattern includes a single candlestick and usually occurs toward the end or during a downward trend. This pattern usually has a small body and an elongated lower shadow during its trading range. Whenever this pattern appears at the bottom of a down trend, its long wick represents an unsuccessful effort by bears to keep the price down, and at the same time, the bulls are trying to increase the price. It usually suggests the end of a downward trend and the beginning of a rather bullish reversal in the market.

Morning Star

It consists of three candlesticks and is believed to be a bullish sign in the market. So, it essentially is a buy signal for all traders. It usually forms after a market's downward trend and signifies the beginning of an upward trend. In a way, the morning star pattern suggests a reversal of the previous price trend. This pattern indicates that a trend is changing from bearish to bullish.

Bullish Engulfing

This pattern represents a major defeat for the sellers.

When the second candlestick bar opens, the sellers are already pushing the prices below the close of the previous candlestick. You might think that the bears are winning, but the buyers will step in to begin buying aggressively. Not only are they able to reverse the direction from the open, but they also manage to push the prices higher than before.

The Bullish Engulfing Pattern is an excellent reversal indicator, but you must always keep looking for subsequent price action and other indicators to confirm the reversal. If prices trade below the pattern again, maybe the pattern failed.

Harami

It is a simple pattern consisting of two candlesticks that are positioned such that the first one engulfs the second one vertically. There are two inferences you can draw from this pattern. The first one is it indicates an unavoidable increase in volatility. It means the traders have an opportunity to establish trades based on an increase in trade volatility in a specific direction. The second is that this pattern can also be an indication of exhaustion and the onset of a reversal.

Bearish Patterns

Bearish patterns typically form after an uptrend. They signal a point of resistance.

Hanging man

The hanging man is the bearish equivalent of the hammer. Even if shaped like a hammer, the only difference is it only appears toward an uptrend's end. It essentially is a reversal candlestick pattern with a small body and a rather long lower shadow. If there is any weakness in the existing price movement, it can be determined by the hanging man. It means the bulls or the buyers in the market have managed to drive the prices upward but cannot do it beyond a given point.

Bearish Engulfing

If the uptrend in a market reverses, it is represented by a bearish engulfing pattern. The initial candle maintains a small green body that stands engulfed by an ensuing long red candle. It essentially showcases any reduction in the price due to the pressure of bearish investors. It is an indication of an imminent market downturn. The significance of the trend increases when the second candle goes lower.

Evening Star

An evening star pattern uses three candlesticks - a bullish, bearish, and small-bodied candlestick. This pattern is created whenever a short candle is sandwiched between the green and red candlesticks. The evening star pattern is the equivalent of the bullish morning star. Traders commonly use it to determine whether the uptrend will transform into a downtrend or shift in reverse. This pattern is mostly sharp when the third candlestick erases the gains of the first candle.

Three Black Crows

The three black crows candlestick pattern comprises three long red candles. They have short or even no wicks.

This pattern is used to determine if the uptrend will reverse into a downtrend or not. Whenever a trading session begins at a price synonymous with the one on the previous day, but the sellers are bearish and push the price lower, and with each close, this pattern is created. Traders have the option of taking a short position once this pattern appears. To determine whether this pattern has formed or not, technical and volume analysis can be used.

Technical Analysis Indicators

Technical indicators are used to determine the measurements associated with a financial product or security. They can make calculations according to the volume, price, social metrics, or any other indicator available.

Technical analysts generally base their ways and methods on the basic notion that past price patterns can be used to predict price movements in the future. Any trader who uses technical analysis has a variety of technical indicators to choose from. These indicators can be used to identify the likely points of entry and exit.

Technical indicators are categorized as follows -

If they are pointing towards future trends, they will be called leading indicators.

Indicators confirming a pattern that is already underway will be called lagging indicators.

Indicators clarifying real-time events will be called coincident indicators.

There are also overlay indicators that indicate data over price, oscillators that swing between a minimum and maximum value. These indicators are categorized according to the information they present.

Another set of indicators is used to measure and determine a specific aspect of the market known as momentum indicators. The trading strategy chosen by the trader determines the variety of technical indicators he will use.

Leading vs. Lagging Indicators

Leading indicators are used to point towards future events, and lagging indicators are used to confirm something that has already happened.

Leading indicators are generally used for short-term and mid-term analysis. Analysts use them while anticipating a specific trend, and some statistical tools are needed to support their suppositions. Leading indicators come in handy, especially while predicting any market slumps or potential threats of recession. They can also prove useful in trading and technical analysis as they have solid predictive qualities. On the other hand, lagging indicators come in handy if you want to confirm an event or a trend that is in progress or has already occurred. Regardless of the indicator used, they certainly highlight certain features of the market that might not have been identified. When it comes to long-term chart analysis, lagging indicators are commonly used.

Momentum Indicator

As evident in the name, these indicators are commonly used to measure and determine the momentum displayed by the market. It is a measure used to calculate the speed at which price changes in the market. So, momentum indicators are used to measure and determine how quickly prices rise and fall. It is commonly used as a tool in short-term analysis.

Momentum traders usually enter and exit the market when the momentum is increasing and starts fading, respectively. If the market isn't volatile, any price change that occurs is within a small range. An ideal situation for momentum traders is when the volatility increases and there is a sudden movement in the price.

Anyone who invests in short-term opportunities, such as day traders and other short-term traders, usually uses momentum indicators. Scalpers also belong to this category. Their primary aim is to move from one high momentum asset to another while repeating their tried and tested trading plan.

Trading Volume

The trading volume is the metric used to determine the total number of individual units that were traded for a specific asset within a given timeframe. It is believed to be the most helpful indicator.

"Volume precedes price" is a rather popular belief in the world of trading and is believed to be the most significant technical indicator. Regardless of the direction, if the trading volume is large, it is considered to indicate a significant price move. The power of the underlying asset can be measured by using the trading volume. For instance, a move can be validated if high volatility presents itself with high trading volume.

Price levels that had high volumes in the past can be used to determine the ideal points for entry and exit in the market. Ideally, the levels of support and resistance must be present along with high volume. This occurrence confirms the specific strength of a level.

Relative Strength Index (RSI)

The RSI indicator is used to determine a specific asset is oversold or overbought. It essentially measures the momentum of price change to determine the rate at which the price is changing. The data obtained from this index is represented as numbers between 1 and 100 on a line chart.

If the index value is less than 30, the asset is believed to be oversold, while it is said to be overbought if its index value is over 70. If you use using this technique, don't forget to take its readings into consideration with a pinch of salt. It tends to reach extreme values when the market conditions are rather extraordinary and still keep moving in spite of this. It is considered one of the ideal indicators for beginners in trading because it is an easy-to-understand technical indicator.

Moving Average (MA)

Moving Averages makes it easier for traders to identify any trends in the market by smoothing out price action. The averages do not have predictive qualities as they are based on past price data. Therefore, they are known as lagging averages. The price data from previous periods or historical price data is used to calculate the moving average.

Moving Average Convergence Divergence (MACD)

The Moving Average Convergence Divergence makes use of two moving averages to display the market's momentum and is, therefore, an oscillator. This tracks and monitors already occurred price actions and is, therefore, a lagging indicator. It consists of two lines known as the signal line and the MACD line. The MACD is used to understand the relationship between the two lines. Any event present at the crossover between these lines is notable. If the MACD line is above the signal line where it crosses the other, it indicates a bullish market while it indicates a bearish market if the MACD line's crossover point is under the signal line.

Fibonacci Retracement Tool

The Fibonacci Retracement tool or Fib Retracement tool is a prominent indicator. It is established on a string of numbers known as the Fibonacci sequence. These digits were developed in the 13th century by Leonardo Fibonacci, a mathematician of Italian descent. These numbers are commonly used as indicators in technical analysis. The ratios obtained from Fibonacci numbers are used by the Fibonacci Retracement tool and converted into percentages. These are later plotted on a chart that traders use to determine points of potential resistance and support.

These Fibonacci ratios are:

0%

23.6%

38.2%

61.8%

78.6%

100%

Numerous traders also deem 50% to be a Fibonacci tool. Furthermore, any ratios outside the usual range of 0-100% can be considered too. 161.8%, 261.8%, and 423.6% are the most common ones.

The general idea of calculating and plotting percentage ratios on a price chart is to determine any points of interest in the market. Traders usually select two price points on the chart. After this, the 0 and 100 values of the Fibonacci Retracement tool are pinned at the previously selected points. It essentially helps them determine the stop-loss range that is present between the two points. This information can be used to determine the right time for entry and exist based on the potential offered to the traders.

Stochastic RSI

As evident from the name, the StochRSI indicator is derived from RSI. Just like RSI, its primary aim is to predict if an underlying asset is overbought or oversold in the market. However, unlike the RSI, the StochRSI is not produced from price data. It is generated from RSI values. The values of StochRSI usually lie between the numbers 0 and 1 on charting tools. If the StochRSI value is close to either the upper or lower extreme of the given range, it is believed to be the most helpful. The StochRSI is challenging to understand because of its speed and high sensitivity, producing several false signals.

If the StochRSI of an asset is more than 0.8, it is believed to be overbought. It may be considered oversold when the indicator is below 0.2. That said, these indicators must never be used as the sole sign to enter or exit trades in the market. Several other factors are at play, and they cannot be overlooked. When combined with other techniques of market analysis, technical analysis offers the best results.

Bollinger Bands

The Bollinger bands are titled after John Bollinger and are used to assess market volatility. They are used to determine if an asset is oversold or overbought. It consists of three bands plotted on a chart accompanied by the price action of an asset. As the volatility in the market changes, the gap between the bands also expands and contracts accordingly. If the market price of an asset is close to the upper band, the asset is likely to be overbought in the market. On the other hand, it is believed the asset is likely to be oversold if the existing price is closer to the lower band on the chart.

Volume-Weighted Average Price

The volume-weighted average price (VWAP) method combines price action with the strength of volume. VWAP is used to determine the standard price of the asset for a period based on its weighted volume. This is obtained by considering the price levels that experienced the highest volume in terms of trading. It is commonly used as a measure to determine the existing market conditions. If the market price is above the VWAP line, the market is bullish, and it is bearish when below this line.

You can use the VWAP to identify areas that offer higher liquidity.

Parabolic SAR

If you want to discern the direction in which the trend is moving or any likely reversals, use the Parabolic SAR. SAR is an acronym for Stand and Reverse. It is usually used to identify the point ideal for opening a short position and closing a long position or the other way round. It is typically represented as a sequence of dots on the price chart and appears either above or below the current price. If this sequence is present above the price, it shows a downtrend. It essentially means the market is bearish, and it is a sell signal. Similarly, if the dots are present below the price, it represents an uptrend, or the market is bullish. If the asset is moving upward, it is an ideal time to buy. A reversal happens if the dots flip to the other side of the chart.

This is used to identify the general orientation of the market trends and for identifying any reversals. Traders commonly use it to establish their profit targets and creating stop losses. It helps traders protect their investments or profits.

Ichimoku Cloud

This indicator is a combination of several indicators presented on one chart and is believed to be more complex than others. In the beginning, it might seem quite overwhelming and tricky to understand, given all the different formulae involved in it and its complex working mechanism. However, as with any new skill, it simply takes time to get the hang of it.

The Ichimoku Cloud can be used to gain insights into different conditions prevalent in the market, including the momentum of assets and the levels of support or resistance along with the direction in which the trends are moving. All the five essential averages are calculated and are plotted on a chart. This simple representation of data makes it easier for traders to consider and analyze. Ichimoku Cloud is used to forecast any likely resistance and support areas by producing a "cloud" using these averages. The traders use this indicator as it produces distinct and well-defined trading signals.

The market is said to be on an uptrend if the current price is overhead of the cloud. Similarly, the market is in a downtrend if the current price is under the cloud. This tool can be used for strengthening any other trading indications too.

Technical Analysis Strategies

Technical analysis helps to predict price movements by analyzing historical content, such as price and volume.

Technical analysis is usually used to make predictions of price movements using historical data such as trade price and volume. It includes two methods of technical analysis known as the top-down approach and the bottom-up approach. Short-term traders prefer the former, while long-term traders usually opt for the latter.

The Top-Down Approach

This method of analysis doesn't concentrate only on individual securities and instead looks at how the overall economy is doing. It is essentially a tool for macroeconomic analysis. Traders using the top-down approach focus on short-term gains.

The Bottom-Up Approach

This does not have a macroeconomic view and focuses on individual securities. Investors intend to hold a long-term view on their trades and seek value in their decisions use this approach.

The form of technical analysis used may be different for different traders. For instance, trend lines and volume indicators are often favored by day traders. On the other hand, swing traders commonly use technical indicators or chart patterns to make trading decisions. Some traders might opt for a combination of technical and volume indicators before making any decisions.

Algorithms Used

Create a Trading System

A well-made scheme is important so that you do not make critical decisions at the last moment. So, before you can start trading, spend some time and create a trading system you wish to follow.

Identify Securities

There is no hard and fast rule that the plan you have created or strategy you have opted for will be ideal for all securities. The parameters must change according to the security you want to invest in.

Find the Right Brokerage

Now that you are aware of the security you want, it is time to find a brokerage. It must offer the needed functions for monitoring the chosen technical indicators. It should also keep the costs low so that it does not take away valuable profits.

Track and Monitor Trades

The functionality required would depend on the strategy traders choose. A basic account is a low-cost option, while a margin account is needed for day traders.

Use Additional Tools

In order to maximize performance, other features might be necessary. This depends on the requirements of the trader. For instance, some might require instant access on the go or mobile alerts, while others might opt for automated systems for executing trades.

Chapter Four: Basics of Cryptocurrency

Cryptocurrencies are currencies that do not have a centralized lender like a country's central bank. They are created using computer encryption techniques that limit the number of monetary units (or coins) created and then verify any transfer of the funds after their creation.

This creation technique is known as "mining" due to its theoretical similarity to mining gold or other precious metals. To mine cryptocurrency, one needs to solve an increasingly complex algorithm or puzzle. Solving these algorithms takes a lot of computer processing power. In other words, it costs money to mine them, so we can't just create value out of thin air. Therefore, these currencies and their value are secured by the laws of mathematics as opposed to any central government or bank.

As cryptocurrency adoption increases, so does the number of real-world uses. Everything from physical goods, gift cards, tickets to sports games, and even hotel bookings can be purchased using cryptocurrency. Certain bars and restaurants have now also started accepting it as a means of payment. Some NGOs now accept donations in Bitcoin and other cryptocurrencies as well. There are also more illicit uses, with the cases of underground online marketplaces dealing in illegal goods, such as Silk Road and AlphaBay. These currencies have a huge number of advantages versus the currencies that we know and use today. This is what makes them so attractive to both long-term investors and short-term speculators.

Despite popular belief, Bitcoin was not the first cryptocurrency. E-gold was introduced in 1996, 12 years before Satoshi Nakamoto released the Bitcoin white paper. E-gold was backed by actual gold reserves and, at its height, had over a million users. It was anonymous, and because the banking system was not yet adapted to the digital world, criminals were easily able to use it for crimes like identity theft and money laundering. E-gold also operated centrally, which made the system a prime target for hackers. The US government forcibly shut it down.

Other forms of cryptocurrency have come into existence, some of which you may have used. People can purchase Facebook credits to enable certain games and programs on Facebook or to beef up their Farmville. Microsoft Rewards is a program that rewards people with digital points for using certain services. These are actually cryptocurrencies!

Bitcoin, however, was a game-changer because it introduced a new technology: blockchain. In fact, blockchain was designed specifically for the implementation of the Bitcoin protocol. A blockchain is a decentralized software, meaning that, unlike e-gold, it is not operated by any one entity. Rather, its operation is spread across thousands of node computers across the globe. This decentralization has many benefits. One is that hacking is virtually impossible, as there is no central server to break into. A hacker would have to control 51% of the nodes in the blockchain! Another benefit is that the information it contains cannot be manipulated or tampered with without, again, controlling 51% of the Blockchain's nodes. This implies that the info saved on a blockchain is immutable. It cannot be changed. New protocols can be implemented through something called a fork, but the information stored in the blockchain is there permanently.

The key to Bitcoin's success is that it eliminated the problem of double-spending. Double spending is the process whereby the same token is spent twice, which enables fraudulent transactions. The verification process that Nakamoto created involves something called proof of work, which prevents double-spending.

New dollars are created either by the government raising or lowering interest rates or by printing new money (this actually leads to inflation). New tokens of cryptocurrency can only be created when people actually use them. Some cryptocurrencies, like the XRP, are programmed so that no new ones can ever be created, and the only ones that will ever be in existence were created when the program first launched. Most, however, use the process of mining to create new tokens.

Mining is the procedure where cryptocurrency transactions get confirmed, so the growth in supply remains consistent with the demand. Therefore, the value is more natural than that of the dollar, whose value is manipulated by the government. Clearly, cryptocurrency is money, arguably a truer, more authentic form of money than traditional dollars.

Blockchain

The blockchain is a list of transactions that continues to grow every day. The blocks on the blockchain are linked to transactions completed on cryptocurrency platforms such as Ethereum or Bitcoin. Every block contains a hash pointer that causes it to be connected to the block that comes before it. A timestamp is going to be attached to each transaction so that the users can tell when the deal was accepted into the chain.

You will find the first work with secure blockchains happened in the early '90s by Stuart Haber and W. Scott Stornetta. Both students were working with Merkle trees to see if they could find a more efficient way to gather data from a single block.

The first distribution of blockchain was conceptualized by someone associated with the Satoshi Nakamoto group back in 2008. They did this while working on the core components for Bitcoin's public ledger. The blockchain is tied to a peer-to-peer network that will be distributed through a server once a timestamp has been placed on a transaction.

The database for blockchain is managed autonomously. So, while you are using the blockchain for cryptocurrencies like Bitcoin, you are guaranteed that there is not going to be any double-spending occurring unless you or an administrator says that it is all right.

Someone in the Nakamoto group used the word blockchain in a paper for the first time when it was published in 2008. It was from there that the term went on to describe a cryptocurrency platform. In 2014, the file for Bitcoin's blockchain was 20 GB. Right now, the record sits at over 100 GB.

Blockchain 2.0 was a term that was used when describing the new application that would take place on the distributed Blockchain's database. It was described as a language that you would be able to program to write smart contracts in a sophisticated manner. Once the smart contract was written out, and then an invoice would be created so that payment could be delivered once the critical terms of the agreement were carried out. The blockchain 2.0 technologies went beyond transactions and made exchanges that would end up acting as an arbiter for money and data.

When blockchain was created, it was expected that people could be excluded from the global economy by turning on privacy protection that would allow people to monetize their information while being provided the capability of ensuring that the creators were compensated for their intellectual property.

Blockchain's second-generation made it so that a user's digital id and persona could be stored, all while providing an avenue that would assist in solving the problem of social inequality. In 2016, a new protocol was implemented where an off-chain oracle would be empowered to gain access to data and events that are not on the network so that it can predict the market's conditions for blockchain to interact with the market accordingly.

The Russian Federation announced that they were going to be implementing a project with Blockchain's platform when it came to electronic voting. The music industry has been using blockchain as well to issue royalties and keep track of copyrights.

The blocks on the blockchain that are not selected to be included in the chain are called orphan blocks. Peers are going to support the multiple versions of the blocks throughout time. Only the highest-scoring version will be kept since they will be overwritten inside the database before retransmitted to their peers for improvement. There won't be any guarantee that the block's entry will be kept. However, this is going to make it to where the blocks will not be writing over each other and causing duplicate data to be placed on the blockchain.

Whenever data is stored on a network, the blockchain is going to eliminate the risks of keeping your information in one place. Since the blockchain is decentralized, you are going to use ad hoc messages on the distributed network.

Blockchain's network is going to lack the vulnerable points that hackers can exploit in a centralized system. Blockchain's security will include methods like public-key cryptography. Public keys are a random string of letters and numbers that identify each user. The public key is going to be sent out to someone who wants to send you coins.

The value tokens sent out across a blockchain network will record anything tied to that address. Private keys are going to have a password tied to them so that users can access their assets that other people cannot get into. You are going to need to keep your private key to yourself because if someone else has that key, they will have half of what they need to gain access to your digital currency and other assets.

Another way to think about private and public keys is your phone number and your passcode to your phone. Your phone number is the public key because there will be people that know it, but the passcode to your phone is private so that no one can get into your phone.

Centralized systems are controlled by a central authority and will experience data manipulation. But, whenever a system is decentralized, it will make it to the point where everyone on the network can see the data that is there, which means that there is nothing hidden from the users.

Every node that is on the blockchain system is going to have a copy of the blockchain. The database and computational trust will maintain the quality of data. There will be no centralized copy that will exist, which implies there won't be one user trusted more than another. Transactions are going to be broadcast on the network for everyone to see. The messages that are sent out on a best effort basis, mining nodes are going to work at validating transactions and creating blocks before a broadcast is sent out from that block to the nodes so that the operation can be verified, and then a block can be built from another node. There will be timestamp schemes that are used by blockchain so that the system can serialize changes. Two other schemes that are used by blockchain are proof of stake and evidence of burn.

The blockchain will keep growing and will be accompanied by a risk of node centralization because of computer resources required to operate the bigger data files, which will become more expensive.

Cryptocurrency and Fiat Currency

Thousands of years ago, shells, beads, and grains were acceptable currencies in a bartering society. As technology became more advanced and governments expanded their influence, money evolved in relevance and power. Today, much of the world's money is based upon a Fiat system where banknotes and coins are assigned a value in accordance with the government they represent. The value assigned to a nation's money is linked more to that nation's influence than on tangible items, such as silver and gold. Money is as political as it is economic.

During the American Civil War, the Confederate States printed their own paper money in a show of defiance to the Union and to help legitimize their campaign. Once the Union won the war, however, the confederate banknotes were quickly put out of circulation.

Regardless of what type of banknote a person may hold, it is generally agreed that there are two primary attributes of a successful currency. These features are:

Utilizing money as a means of exchange

Using money to store and denote value

For money to fulfill these roles, the people who use the money must maintain a certain level of trust in the currency and the entities that regulate it. This brings us back to my initial assertion that Money is dead. Or rather, the modern interpretation and control of fiat money are dead.

As in the earlier example of the American Civil War, money becomes obsolete when it is no longer held as an acceptable form of currency. It cannot be traded for goods, services, and debts, and the government backing it does not have sufficient influence to assign value. The general populace loses faith, and the money dies.

Now, let's turn our attention to what we consider contemporary fiat money. In the 1970s, the U.S. dollar was taken off the Gold Standard, with the economy itself being used as the barometer the government utilized to assign value. More money could be printed, and inflation could be manipulated to an even higher degree. With the introduction of the Information Age, money became digital. What once could be buried in the backyard for safekeeping or transported across territory lines via coach and wagon could now traverse miles and nations in a virtual blink. "Cash" money became an inconvenience. It's too bulky to carry around large amounts, easily misplaced, and more difficult to exchange for another currency.

Converting our modern money to a digital platform is the next logical progression. However, it also comes with virtual disadvantages. No, there aren't any Wild West outlaws saddling up to your local 'Western Union' and threatening to shoot up the town if not given a wire transfer. No, the villain is more ominous and faceless. Every day, companies and banks are attacked by hackers and identity thieves whose goal is to reroute those monetary zeros and commas from one place to another. What's worse, these virtual outlaws are outpacing the governments tasked with protecting money.

Established entities find it difficult to counteract these attacks and instead spend resources (i.e., your money) to clean up the aftermath. This comes along with the continual manipulation of money for economic and political gain. The public's trust in the value of modern currency and its protection has been diminishing for some time now. People are ready for the next iteration of money. They want a faster, safer currency and one not so easily manipulated by the proverbial "talking heads." It was this progression of thought that led to the conception of cryptocurrency.

The currencies we use in everyday life are called 'fiat' by the people involved in cryptocurrency. Despite the word 'currency' in the word cryptocurrency, there are greater similarities between cryptocurrencies and stocks than cryptocurrencies and fiat currencies. A purchase of cryptocurrency is a purchase of a technology stock, an entry in a digital ledger called a blockchain, and a part of the digital network for that cryptocurrency.

Common Cryptocurrencies

Bitcoin

Bitcoin was created in January 2009, and its concept was first published in a whitepaper by someone named Satoshi Nakamoto. To date, no one is aware of the identity of this person since the paper was published using a pseudonym. It could also be that multiple people created Bitcoin and used a single name on the paper. Bitcoin became famous because of its low transaction fees as well as its ability to bypass governments. Its decentralization method ensures that no one person controls the whole system, and that is what appealed to most people who originally joined the Bitcoin bandwagon. By market capitalization, Bitcoin is the biggest cryptocurrency in the world.

Ethereum

Blockchain technology isn't just associated with Bitcoin. It would be erroneous for one to think that Bitcoin is the only form of cryptocurrency in existence. Bitcoin is one of several hundreds of applications that make use of Blockchain technology in the present day.

Ethereum is another open software platform that is founded on Blockchain technology. It allows developers to create and deploy applications that are also decentralized in nature.

People tend to think that Ethereum and Bitcoin are completely alike – this is not true. Ethereum and Bitcoin do share facts such as they are both public, distributed Blockchain networks. But it must be noted that their major difference lies in their purpose and ability. Bitcoin provides one precise application of Blockchain technology based on a peer-to-peer digital cash system. This system allows online Bitcoin transactions to take place. The Bitcoin blockchain is used to keep track of all Bitcoin transactions that are made on the platform. In the Ethereum blockchain, it is used to run the program code of any decentralized application that is developed on the platform.

In the Bitcoin system, miners mine for Bitcoin. In the Ethereum system, miners mine for Ether. Ether keeps the network running. Developers use the tokens to pay services or fees on the Ethereum platform. This token can be used as a tradable digital currency.

For Ethereum to work, the platform requires at least several thousands of people to run the software on their computers – this powers the network. Every computer, also known as a node in the network, runs something known as the EVM (Ethereum Virtual Machine). The EVM can be considered an operating system that comprehends and executes the software written in a programming language specific to Ethereum.

Ripple

As mentioned earlier, cryptocurrency technology is based on decentralization. However, ripple takes a more traditional approach. It takes the SWIFT transactions banking idea and utilizing blockchain technology, and it provides a much-needed upgrade.

Currently, sending traditional currencies via SWIFT goes through several intermediaries and takes several days. The process is less secure and riskier than what Ripple has to offer. On the other hand, ripple provides instant and cheaper transactions that are activated using a single currency, XRP. Currently, over 100 banks worldwide work with the Ripple team, including ATB Financial, CIBC, UBS, Standard Chartered, etc.

Monero

Monero allows users to send and receive funds without a public transaction record available on the blockchain. All Monero transactions are private by default. If you believe in privacy first and foremost, then Monero ticks all the boxes. The currency is designed to be fully anonymous and untraceable. This goes as far as their development team, which, unlike other coins, has no public CEO or figurehead.

Monero also uses "ring signatures," a special type of cryptography to ensure untraceable transactions. This allows users to receive money without being able to link the address to the sender. This could be looked at as both a positive or negative depending on your viewpoint regarding anonymity. The ring signatures also conceal the transaction amount, in addition to the identity of the buyer and seller. Unlike Dash, Monero has been open source from its inception so that anyone can view the software code for total transparency.

The anonymity of the currency has made it a favorite of the dark web. Before its shutdown, Darknet market site

AlphaBay had adopted Monero as well as Bitcoin to process transactions. Everything from illegal drugs, weaponry, and stolen credit cards were traded on the platform. Its anonymity has also made Monero a favorite among ransomware hackers.

We will have to wait and watch if Monero will branch out to more legitimate use, such as to conceal one's true net worth or if it will live on to be the favorite coin of more illicit industries, preventing it from mass adoption versus other coins. This uncertainty could be used to the speculator's advantage as they seek to profit from mass adoption potential.

Factom

Like Ethereum, Factom expands on ways to use blockchain technology outside of just currency. While Ethereum is based on two-way verification and ensuring contracts are unbreakable, Factom promises to do the same with large blocks of data by providing a record system that cannot be tampered with. This would allow businesses, governments to provide a track record of data without alteration or loss. The practical applications for this include legal applications, company accounts, medical records, and even voting systems. Just imagine a world where it was physically impossible to rig elections or where an accounting scandal like Enron couldn't happen again.

Like other projects utilizing blockchain, Factom cannot be altered because no single person runs the network. The network is collectively owned by millions of users, independently of each other. While data owned by one person is prone to malevolence, hacking, user error, and alteration, the same is not possible with data owned by an entire network.

With regards to investing, like Ether is to Ethereum, Factoids are the "currency" of the Factom system. The more applications that are generated using Factom, the more these Factoids are worth. Factom has already secured a deal with consulting firm iSoftStone to provide blockchain-based administration software projects for cities in China. The deal includes plans for auditing and verification services.

Like other blockchain technology, common questions surrounding Factom are ones of scalability and wider technology adoption. The other main drawback to Factom investing is whether the team can run the system at a consistent profit going forward - or whether the technology will lead to a race to the bottom in terms of price.

Dogecoin

You can't talk about Blockchain without mentioning Dogechain, the official Blockchain explorer of Dogecoin. It is definitely one of the most historical cryptocurrencies around and is a peer-to-peer, open-source currency— meaning its use is free for everyone.

Often, Dogecoin is called the Internet Currency. After all, it was named after "Doge," that famous Shiba-Inu that you can find in most memes everywhere. The Dogecoin Wallet is then found on the Internet — which you could then access from either your computer or any other mobile devices that you are using. While it initially uses US Dollars, users are also allowed to have those dollars converted into other currencies for smoother transactions.

To make use of Dogechain, you'd first have to go to the Dogecoin Website. There, you will be asked whether you want your Dogecoin wallet to be on your Desktop, Online, on Your Phone, or even on a Paper Wallet.

Once you have made your choice, you'd then be asked to choose the Operating System (OS) of your computer— either Windows, OS X, or Android, and you would then be given instructions as to how to access the wallet.

After following the given instructions earlier, you will be asked to download the wallet. You would see a link on the screen, so all you'd have to do is click the link and then have the wallet installed on your device. Once you have finished with the downloading and installation, you can then use your wallet. You probably just have to wait for at least 1 to 5 minutes for it to synchronize on all your devices, then you're all set.

Golem

Golem is a coin token based on Ethereum blockchain technology. Described by some commentators as the "Airbnb of computing," the value of the coin is centered on the software that can be developed using it.

The founders of the Golem Project refer to it as a "supercomputer," with the ability to interconnect with other computers for various purposes. These include scientific research, data analysis, and cryptocurrency mining. For example, if your computer has unused power, using the Golem network, you can rent that power (therefore the Airbnb comparison) to someone else who needs it. The user who needs the extra power has the ability to access supercomputer levels of processing power for a fraction of the cost of actually owning the processing power themselves.

The ability for users to earn money for their unused computing power is, in theory, a no-brainer. However, what remains to be seen is the practical application of the technology. The Golem team's lack of marketing visibility has also appeared to hurt the coin's value in recent times. The lack of ability to buy GNT using fiat currency (such as USD) is also a drawback for the mass market.

Chapter Five: Getting Started

To invest and trade in cryptocurrencies, you have first to learn how to store and buy them. Almost all cryptocurrencies are stored, bought, and traded in the same manner, so we will look at Bitcoin as an example to understand the process.

Acquiring

The most popular way to acquire Bitcoins is through computer mining. Although this is not the cheapest or easiest way, it does result in you earning free Bitcoin from your mining practices. It is a system of complex mathematical equations that are solved by computers. This is how Bitcoins were originally created and how more continue to enter circulation. At the time of this publication, there are approximately 25 Bitcoins mined every 10 minutes using these complex computers and their mathematical equations.

Another way to get access to Bitcoins, which is much easier, is to find a Bitcoin exchange and simply purchase them. Take your time and find an exchange where you won't be scammed. Avoid any company or individual claiming that they will assist you in mining Bitcoin, especially if it seems too good or anything with a generally bad feel to it. Ideally, you should be able to research the Bitcoin exchange in question and discover a great deal of information about it right away.

Make sure you always research the exchange so that you can be sure you are not being ripped off. Due to the high value of Bitcoin these days, many people use it as a chance to scam individuals out of their funds, and you do not want to be a victim. One other thing worth noting is pyramid schemes that involve Bitcoin. While these may sound profitable or like they will assist you with investing, they will not save you money, and they will also likely result in you not having any Bitcoin in the end.

Despite how many scams exist out there surrounding Bitcoin, you must understand that this is not worth completely abandoning the Bitcoin currency over. Recall that even traditional currencies can result in scams, yet they are still highly valuable and essential to daily life in our society. Bitcoins are not as necessary to our daily life, but they are still highly valuable and can provide a great deal of return and wealth to those who purchase them or invest in them.

The best thing to do is ensure that you are using credible and legitimate sources from which to purchase your Bitcoin. Once you have identified a sound exchange to invest in, you can begin freely investing in as many Bitcoin as you desire. This is the easiest and safest way to become involved in owning and trading Bitcoin without having to fear that you will be scammed or otherwise ripped off in the world of cryptocurrencies.

Cryptocurrency Exchanges

A cryptocurrency exchange is an online platform that facilitates the buying, selling, and exchange of cryptocurrencies for other cryptocurrencies or conventional fiat currencies like dollars and pounds. There are different kinds of cryptocurrency exchanges, each serving different kinds of people according to their specific needs. If you aim to trade professionally with access to sophisticated trading tools, advanced exchanges allow you to do that. Most of these will need you to verify your identity before you can set up a trading account. For those looking for a one-time or occasional trade, there are simple exchanges that allow you to trade without having to set up a trading account. There are three types of exchanges:

Trading platforms

These platforms connect traders and charge a fee for each transaction. They play the role of an escrow, holding both cryptocurrencies and fiat money and handling the processing of orders and trades.

Direct Trading Platforms

These also are known as peer-to-peer markets. Unlike trading platforms, which act as intermediaries, direct trading platforms allow buyers and sellers to trade directly. Direct trading platforms have no fixed market price. Exchange rates are determined exclusively by sellers.

Brokers and Direct Commercial Exchanges

These are websites that work in a similar manner to foreign exchange brokers. They allow anyone to easily buy cryptocurrencies at fixed prices that are determined by the exchange itself.

Picking an Exchange

There are a lot of options that you can pick from when it comes to deciding on a cryptocurrency exchange. However, you should not join an exchange because it happens to be the first one you stumbled upon. Before joining an exchange, take the following factors into consideration.

Fees

Cryptocurrency exchanges charge users transaction, deposit, and withdrawal fees. This is what keeps them in business. Fee structures vary from exchange to exchange.

Most common exchanges apply a volume-based fee structure that allows those doing huge trades to pay lower fees. Before joining an exchange, make sure you know everything about their fee structure. Most of this information can be easily found on the exchange's website.

Payment Methods

Before joining an exchange, find out the available payment methods and see if they are convenient for you. Remember that using credit cards and PayPal will mean an extra charge, while bank transfers might take longer before you get your cryptocurrency.

Verification Requirements

Cryptocurrency exchanges in the U.K and the U.S. will require identity verification before a person can deposit and withdraw funds, while others allow for complete anonymity. Although verification might seem like it goes against the spirit of cryptocurrencies, it helps protect the exchange against money laundering and scams.

Geographical Restrictions

Some exchanges may have functions that are only accessible from within specific geographic regions or countries. Before joining an exchange, make sure it offers full support in your country.

Exchange Rates

Different cryptocurrency exchanges have different exchange rates. Look around different exchanges to find out which one offers the best price for the cryptocurrency you intend to trade in.

Different Exchanges

Described below are the five most accepted cryptocurrency exchanges based on various factors, including user reviews, security, fee structure, accessibility, and user-friendliness.

Coinbase

This is one of the most well-known exchanges. Started in 2012, it has a good reputation, strong backing from trusted investors, and millions of users. The Coinbase platform is user-friendly and convenient, allowing users to buy, sell, store, and spend securely. Coinbase supports Bitcoin, Ether, and LiteCoin. It also provides a mobile wallet that is available on both Android and iOS. Coinbase is best known for good security, reasonable fees, and user-friendliness. Funds stored on Coinbase also are covered by the Coinbase insurance. However, Coinbase has limited country support, limited payment methods, and their GDAX platform is better suited to technical users.

Kraken

Founded in 2011, this is a San Francisco-based exchange. Kraken has partnered with Fidor to build what will be the best and the world's premier crypto bank. It also has integration with Bloomberg terminals. Kraken allows users to trade Bitcoin and a wide variety of world currencies, including U.S. dollars, Canadian dollars, British pounds, euros, and Japanese yen. Kraken also supports a host of other digital currencies, including Bitcoin, Ethereum, Ethereum Classic, Ripple, Dogecoin, Monero, LiteCoin, Stellar, Zcash, and ICONOMI. Kraken is best known for its good reputation, low deposit and transaction fees, decent exchange rates, rich features, worldwide support, and great user support. Its drawbacks are limited payment methods and an unintuitive interface that is not very suitable for newbies.

Poloniex

Poloniex was established in 2014 and has grown to become one of the world's top cryptocurrency exchanges by trade volume. It allows people to exchange Bitcoin for more than 100 types of altcoins. Creating an account with Poloniex is fast and simple. The platform offers a feature-rich, user-friendly interface with advanced analysis tools for the more advanced users. Among cryptocurrency exchanges, Poloniex has one the lowest trading fees. User support is great, with a chat interface where users can request help from other users. Moderators keep the chat box helpful by deleting any inappropriate comments. Poloniex also offers BTC lending and has an open API. The downside to Poloniex is that it does not support fiat currencies.

Shapeshift

Founded in 2013, Shapeshift is an instant crypto exchange that permits customers to exchange cryptocurrencies for different cryptocurrency exchanges. Shapeshift supports Bitcoin and several other altcoins, including Ethereum, Dash, Dogecoin, Monero, and Zcash. Unfortunately, Shapeshift does not support exchanges between cryptocurrency and fiat. An important advantage of Shapeshift is that it allows people to exchange cryptocurrencies while maintaining a great level of anonymity. Users can exchange cryptocurrencies without having to create an account. It doesn't even hold money in a centralized exchange. Shapeshift has a good reputation, a user-friendly user interface for beginners, reasonable prices, and it supports dozens of cryptocurrencies.

LocalBitcoins

This is the most popular P2P marketplace that connects Bitcoin sellers and buyers within the same city or geographical region, with support for thousands of cities worldwide. With LocalBitcoins, the traders can decide on their preferred mode of payment or even meet up in person to do the trade. The platform allows sellers to determine their own exchange rates while it takes a 1 percent commission for every trade. To maintain the security of the platform, it uses a reputation rank system and maintains a public history of each user's trades. It also has an escrow service that holds funds and only releases them after confirmation by the seller that the trade is complete. Signing up on LocalBitcoins requires no identity verification. It provides a free, beginner-friendly way of purchasing Bitcoins, supports various local currencies depending on the location, and is available worldwide. Its drawback is that it has high exchange rates and is not a very good option for buying large amounts of Bitcoin.

Storing

Much like traditional currency, Bitcoins have a digital "wallet" in which you store them. This wallet is automatically created whenever you purchase your first Bitcoin, and it is held for you from that point forward. Any time you purchase Bitcoin or invest in this cryptocurrency, it will be added to your digital wallet. Similarly, any time you spend the currency, it will be withdrawn from this digital wallet.

Your digital wallet exists in one of two places: either directly on your computer or in the cloud storage system. This wallet operates exactly as your bank would, keeping track of any Bitcoin that enters your wallet and any that leave. You can use this wallet to help you pay for goods, receive or send funds, or even save your Bitcoin funds.

You need to remember that a few dangers can be faced with your digital wallet that cannot be reversed should they happen. For example, the wallet is not insured by the FDIC, so should you have any discrepancies or lose any of your funds, you won't be allowed to retrieve them or revive them with any insurance. Furthermore, there are things worth noting about where you choose to store the wallet, as well. For wallets that are stored in the cloud, some companies may have the power to take more Bitcoin than you have approved. As well, servers could be hacked, and the hacker themselves could steal your Bitcoin. However, if you store your wallet on your computer, it can be hacked or damaged with viruses, or they could be deleted or lost should your computer ever fail.

Wallet Types

Different types of wallets are available, and the features that they offer and their compatibility with devices vary as well. Wallets are categorized as hot or cold. Those wallets associated with the Internet or are available online are called hot, while those wallets available offline or aren't associated with the Internet are called cold.

Desktop Wallets

These wallets are applications that can be installed or downloaded onto your laptop or your PC. These wallets will be accessible only from a single device, the one on which they have been downloaded. Desktop wallets offer the highest level of security. However, they will be vulnerable if your computer gets hacked or is attacked by a virus. In such a case, you might end up losing all your funds. Desktop wallets are available for different types of OS like Windows, macOS, and Ubuntu.

Mobile Wallet

A wallet that will run from an app downloaded on your smartphone is referred to as a mobile wallet. This offers convenience and ease of access. These are relatively smaller and simple to use when compared to desktop wallets. Different wallets are available for various operating systems like Android, Windows, and iOS.

Online Wallet

It is a web-based wallet and doesn't have a downloadable app. It is available as data that is stored in a real or virtual server, like the Cloud. It can, therefore, be accessed from any computing device from any location. Some hybrid wallets allow encryption of the private data before it is sent to an online server. Some online wallets have provisions for the storage of private keys online and are controlled by third parties, thereby making them vulnerable to hacking and theft.

Exchange-Hosted Wallet

This is managed by an exchange or a brokerage like Coinbase or Poloniex, for instance. This is different from the wallets mentioned above because you aren't in control of the private keys to your Cryptocurrency stored in them. You will have to place your trust fully in the exchange that is managing it. These wallets do offer services like sending and receiving payments. However, it isn't a wallet in the strict sense of the word. When it comes to managing a lot of funds, it will be better if you make use of any other type of wallet. Exchanges offer convenience by getting rid of the responsibility of securing and backing up the private keys, but this convenience comes at a high cost. Exchanges tend to be the prime targets of hackers. This is quite evident from the failure of two major Bitcoin exchanges like Mt. Gox and Bitfinex.

Hardware Wallets

A hardware wallet is the best way to store all your Cryptocurrency. They are small USB-enabled devices for storing your private keys. The advantage of this wallet is that it is unhackable. They are devised in a manner that they can run the wallet software along and nothing else. This makes them immune to malware that the other wallets can fall prey to. However, the only drawback tends to be their cost. These wallets are a little costly, but they are worth the investment.

Paper Wallets

Another cold storage wallet option that you have is to print or even write down the private key on a piece of paper and then lock this up in a safe or a deposit box. You can print the QR code of your public and private keys. This will help you in sending and receiving digital currency by using a paper wallet. This method eliminates the need to store digital data about your cryptocurrency. Online tools can provide key pairs directly on your system, and this can make your keys vulnerable if the site gets hacked. You can also generate keys by using the command line, provided you have the required cryptographic packages installed in the preferred language. If you lose your private key, there is no way to retrieve it once again. If it is gone, then it is gone for good. So, create multiple copies of the QR code and stash them in different secure spots.

Online Wallets

Block.io

This provides a multi-signature wallet to all cryptocurrency users. This means that for a transaction to be authorized, two or more signatures will be required. One will be the signature of the user, and the other will be the signature of the company. This also implies that the private keys of every wallet will be stored by the team operating at Block.io, and this might be a turn-off for a lot of people. However, it offers more convenience since it supports an HD wallet. It supports the functions of both Bitcoin and Dogecoin.

Exodus

This wallet supports different cryptocurrencies like Bitcoin, Dash, Ether, Dogecoin, and Golem as well. It offers full control to the user over their private keys. It is an open-source wallet.

LoafWallet

If you have a device that can support iOS, this will be a good option. It has all the features that an investor will want. A good mobile wallet will cater to the needs of novice and experienced users, and LoafWallet does this. This is a lightweight client, and you don't need to spend hours syncing it with the Blockchain. It makes use of AES hardware encryption and app sandboxing to prevent anyone from inserting their address into a given transaction. What's more? It can be installed on your Apple Watch as well. If you are looking for functionality, then this is a pretty good option.

Electrum-LTC

This is a popular wallet amongst Bitcoin users. It makes use of a set passphrase for protecting a wallet and for restoring a wallet from a backup. It can be downloaded for devices supported by Linux, Windows, and OSX from the official online site. This is a lightweight wallet, and therefore you needn't wait for hours to sync it with the blockchain. The main advantage of this wallet is its backup feature. Even if the user loses their Electrum-LTC wallet, it can be retrieved in the app using the passphrase. There is an option of generating an offline wallet for cold storage. Users can also export the address of their private key to another wallet.

Trading

In 2018, Nasdaq will begin trading Bitcoin, marking a new chapter in the rise of cryptocurrency. Trading will be particularly lucrative for people who were willing to hold fast through the wild swings in value that the coins present. The general rule is to buy when the price drops and sell when the price increases. Since the values swing so violently throughout the day, traders may make hundreds of trades in just one 24-hour period. Many have found themselves making rather tidy sums of money.

To get started with trading, you have to decide which cryptocurrencies you want to use. Some traders only use one cryptocurrency and base all of their trades on its gains and losses. Others trade between cryptocurrencies to capitalize on trends across the entire crypto-economy. You need a trading platform and decide on the strategies to engage. Starting out by working with an experienced trader until you get used to it can be a great way to learn the most effective trading techniques.

The method of buying and selling Bitcoins differs, because selling isn't as easy as buying. Not to worry yet, you can sell your Bitcoins several ways. You need to find the ideal method for you. This comes with two major options, whereby you can cash out your currency online or in person. It goes without mention that each of the options has its upsides and shortcomings that you need to understand beforehand. Looking at each of them will make the task easier when it comes to deciding the best option to go for in your transaction.

Selling Online

This is the most standard method of selling Bitcoins, and it features two primary methods.

Exchange Trades

This option involves registering with an online exchange and verifying your identity, as we talked about before. However, the best part of exchange trades is that there is little involvement in running the deal. In this case, you only place an order, more like you do with the buy order. You include the type of currency you are selling, the amount, and the price for each unit. If someone comes with a purchase order, the trade will be completed automatically, and you receive the currency into your account.

However, if you are selling Bitcoins for fiat currencies, you may face liquidity and bank issues. This may result in waiting for a considerable amount of time to receive the amount.

Peer-to-Peer Trading Marketplaces

Sites like Purse and Brawker are known to offer these services conveniently. These sites merge people with related needs. Groups include people who want to use Bitcoins to make purchases on sites that do not support the use of digital currencies and those seeking to buy Bitcoins using credit or debit cards. As such, these people can exchange Bitcoins and discounted goods for one another.

The downside involved in the use of online transactions is that this type usually calls for identity verification, which is not as strict for buyers, but more demanding for the sellers. The other concern is the issue of withdrawal of funds, which may be a bit complicated, and take longer than necessary in some cases.

Now, let's see why trading in cryptos can prove financially beneficial!

Chapter Six: Crypto Assets, Why?

Factors Influencing Crypto Assets

As discussed above, the competition in the cryptocurrency market hasn't increased to the level that it's impossible to get in. Crypto assets remain an ideal investment for traders. Many factors influence this theory:

High Accessibility

As most cryptocurrencies are decentralized, the crypto market is available for trading and investment 24/7. This gives investors and traders more freedom in their work. No matter what day it is, even a national holiday, work can resume if they choose to.

Beneficial Enhancement

On trading in a cryptocurrency, you can reap the benefits of both increasing and decreasing prices, while if you buy a cryptocurrency, you would have to wait for when the asset rises in value. Further, for the trading of cryptos, you have a lot of different options to choose from, and even for cryptos themselves, you have a load of options to select which one you want to trade in.

Scope of High Profits

There are possibilities that even if you invest a small amount of capital, it could gain substantial exposure and amplify your deposit. Since there is high volatility in the crypto market, the prices are changing all the time. So, you can make use of these frequent changes in profit to get high returns.

Secure

A transaction made using crypto cannot be reversed. This is good in a sense since every transaction is encrypted, and hackers cannot attain any information about the account or its transactions.

Transparent Transactions

Trading with cryptocurrencies allows you to work faster and without excessive paperwork. It also ensures that you have direct transactions.

Anonymous Usage

As cryptocurrencies give you a fair share of anonymity in any work relating to them, you can ensure that your financial matters are completely confidential. Unlike in cash or credit arrangements, where each transaction is recorded, in crypto transactions, you have privacy.

Trading Over Buying

Trading cryptocurrencies allows you to take a venture on the prices of the assets without actually owning them. If you choose to trade rather than buy, you won't even have to pay a depository or withdrawal sum required if you partake in ownership of the crypto. Trading also gives you a set of freedoms that buying crypto won't.

Types of Trading

Further, there are two types of cryptocurrency trading, based on the time you choose to own the crypto. They are Short-Term trading and Long-Term trading, and both come with their own advantages.

Short-Term Trading

In this type of trading, you possess cryptocurrency for a small time. This time depends on you. When you buy the crypto, you buy it hoping the prices will rise, and when they do, you can sell it when you have an inkling that the prices will drop again. Here are a few advantages of the short-term trading method:

Because of the volatile nature of cryptocurrencies, their prices can increase twofold, even overnight. So, holding on to your crypto for a short time and then selling it when the time is right can give you elevated profits.

Now that the trade and use of cryptocurrencies have gained popularity, more and more cryptos have entered the market. Currently, there are about 1500 cryptos to trade in. This signifies that now there are more than ever opportunities to trade in cryptos and reap financial gains.

Since there are so many cryptos along with so many traders, the market has large trading volumes. For example, if I want to trade my Bitcoins for Dogecoins, I have to find a potential Dogecoin seller to trade with. But since there are so many users in the market, I will definitely find a buyer or seller instantly.

Long-Term trading

In long-term trading, you clasp the crypto for a longer period before selling it. Or, as the traders say, "Hold On for Dear Life." Working on a similar idea as short-term trading uses the volatility of cryptos to believe that in the long game, the cryptocurrency prices will go up. Some pros of this method are:

For long-term trading, you know that you'll be holding on to the crypto for a long time, so you don't have to spend hours on end analyzing the complex market structures.

Once you have bought your cryptocurrency, all you have to do is wait. You don't have to constantly check the rises and dips in the prices as required in the short-term method.

In a long-term way, you don't have to invest large amounts of money. You can buy crypto for a small amount and allow it to increase as time goes by. You also don't have to be worried about small ups and downs in prices, as you're in it for the long run.

What Is HODL?

"Hold On for Dear Life," or HODL was actually initiated from the misspelled word "hold," which in current times refers to the long-time holding of cryptocurrencies. It is a scheme in long-term trading, in which traders buy cryptos and keep them for a long time so that the market values go up and they gain high profits. Traders use this strategy to rule out the possibilities of FUD- Fear, Uncertainty, and Doubt- and FOMO or Fear of Missing Out on opportunities.

So, either way, if you trade in cryptocurrencies and you time your moves right, there is a pretty good chance that you can gain great returns!

Day Trading For a Living

If you do choose to become a day trader, you can either work alone or with a team. Most day traders who work in large institutions or teams tend to have access to direct lines, large volumes of capital, leverage, a trading desk, expensive and mostly accurate software tools, and more. Such traders are only looking to make enough profits for their company and clients. The resources available to them enable them to maximize their profits even if they make risky trades. They can do what an individual trader can never dream of doing.

Single traders regularly manage their own money. They may also take care of another individual's money, but this depends on their capability. They have their own trading desk, but they do maintain contact with a brokerage. These brokerages thrive on commissions and have large volumes of money in their accounts. If they tie up with brokerages, they also get access to the tools and resources used by that brokerage. The scope of these resources is limited, which makes it hard for these day traders to compete with those traders working in large institutions. Since individual traders work alone, they have to take more risks. This indicates their capital needs to be high. They often make their trades basis the technical analysis performed and different day trading strategies. A combination of this analysis and strategy is what enables them to make a profit. They can leverage small market movements.

Day trading does require some complex financial instruments and services, and you need to have the following handy as a day trader. They are:

Multiple News Sources

As a trader, it is essential to follow the news since it has enough information you can leverage to make profits. It is imperative that a day trader is aware when anything significant happens. Trading rooms have information that you need about different stocks, and the news is constantly updated, so you are aware of any real-time changes. These rooms also have access to news organizations such as Dow Jones Newswire, coverage of CNBC and others, and some tools and software to analyze these news sources for any stories.

Access to a Trading Desk

A trading desk is often reserved only for traders who work in large institutions or for people who have a large capital. This capital, as mentioned earlier, is termed as the risk capital that is the amount the trader is willing to lose. The dealing desk will provide these traders with a chance to execute any orders instantly. It is especially important for traders since they tend to focus on stocks that have sharp price movements. For example, if a company were to announce a merger or acquisition, a trader would make profits on the company's stock through arbitrage. These traders can place their orders in the market before other traders to take benefit of the movements in price.

Analytical Software

Most day traders use different trading software, and traders who work with institutions don't purchase them. If you are an individual day trader, bear in mind that these tools are expensive, but many traders who rely on swing trades or technical indicators rely only on these tools. These software have the following attributes:

Broker Integration

Most applications and software work with brokerage companies, and they are linked to the company database. This makes it exceedingly easy for traders to execute any trades they make and eliminates any chance of emotions.

Back testing

When traders choose their strategy, it is critical for them to know how the strategy has worked in the past. This is the only way they can predict how this strategy will work and how it can perform in the future. Bear in mind that the past performance of a strategy does not necessarily indicate the right results since there could be different external factors that influence the functioning of the strategy.

Neural and Genetic Applications

This is a combination of a genetic algorithm and neural network that tracks the movements of the market. This combination makes it easy to generate the perfect strategy to foresee the future price of different stocks.

Automatic Pattern Recognition

These tools can identify different technical indicators in the market based on the flag or channel you key into them. There are some tools that can also identify some complex indicators like the Elliott Wave Pattern.

If you have these software, you have the edge over the other day traders in the market. It is also recommended that you learn how to combine these tools together since that increases the chance of making profits. If you don't know to use the software, learn before you implement it. Most people lose money because they don't know to operate these tools.

Should I Day Trade?

Day trading is difficult and challenging for most people since they are new to trading in cryptocurrencies. You need to learn about the market and the trading world and understand what you are willing to lose before you begin day trading. You need to set the following to determine what you can lose:

Risk capital

Risk tolerance

Goals

If you choose day trading as a career, you will need to spend a lot of your time because you need to practice your strategies if you want to master them. This is the only way you can perfect your strategy and make a lot of money. Day trading cannot be a part-time career, especially if you are trying to trade cryptocurrencies. You need to invest your time and energy fully into this.

If you decide that you are willing to take up the risks that come with day trading, then make sure to start small. Focus on some cryptocurrencies instead of investing directly in the market. If you do the latter, you are going to lose all your money. Do not go all out because that will mess up your strategy and make it hard for you to break even. Ensure you keep your emotions out when you are trading. Maintain a level head when you trade and ensure you focus on your strategy and goal.

Day Trading Strategies

If you want to make profits on frequent and small price movements, developing the right strategy for you is important. An effective and consistent strategy will rely on utilizing charts, patterns, indicators, and technical analysis to predict the movements in price. We will learn some basics a beginner should know. We will also understand things you need to know when you select a day trading strategy. If you learn all this, you will be able to identify the right strategy for you. This strategy is what works best for you in terms of how it suits your trading requirements. If you hire the services of a broker to help you, ensure the following:

Trade automation

Excellent speed

Ability to learn trends from graphs

Profit Orders and Stop-loss limits

Learn about different brokers and understand their companies before you ask someone to take care of the money you want to invest.

Trading Strategies for Beginners

It is difficult for most people to develop the right strategy when they start day trading cryptocurrencies. Ensure you pay attention to the basics and learn the different strategies before you invest. Amateurs often feel they need a complicated approach to succeed. But the simplest strategies yield the best results, so choose one that works for you.

Basics

You must incorporate the following elements into your trading strategy.

Be Consistent

It is difficult to keep emotions at bay when you trade, especially when you look at the screen for a long time. Let the numbers do the talking and ensure you stick to your strategy. Do not, and I repeat, do not let your emotions guide you. You are bound to fail if you listen to them when you trade.

Time Management

This has been mentioned earlier and will be mentioned quite a few times across the book. It is important to learn to manage your time, especially to be a day trader. You must monitor the markets constantly and always be on the lookout for any changes in your trade opportunities.

Create a Demo Account

You need to do this to begin day trading any stocks, including cryptocurrencies. You can use a demo account to test your strategy or even experiment with new strategies. Bear in mind that the practices you use in these demo accounts can help you refine your strategy. Do not expect to make profits even if you have the right strategy. Instead, create numerous demo accounts and practice as much as you can before you invest in cryptocurrencies.

Money Management

Before you begin to trade, you must sit down and assess your financial situation. You should know how much money you can afford to risk. Remember, successful traders never invest more than 2% of their capital. You must also prepare yourself to make some losses.

Timing

The price of cryptocurrencies, like other stocks, is going to fluctuate when the market opens and right before it closes. You must capitalize on these price fluctuations to make a profit. Every experienced day trader is aware of how to read these trends and patterns and uses those to make profits. If you are a beginner, take some time and practice your strategies. Understand the market and make purchases at the right time.

Components for Every Strategy

No matter which type of strategy you choose to use, you need to consider the following components. These components are what make the strategy profitable or not. If your strategy does not include these components, you are going to make losses, and this is something you should accept. Let us understand these components better.

Volatility

Using the volatility component, you can define the profit range for yourself. If your volatility is high, you can maximize the profit you make. It is best to use these volatility limits in the cryptocurrency trading market since they are very volatile.

Liquidity

The liquidity component is a good indicator for when you should enter or exit any position in the market. You will exit the position at a stable price that will allow you to make a profit. A liquid strategy often focuses on stocks of crude oil, gold, and natural gas.

Volume

You can use this component to understand the number of times a specific cryptocurrency will change or was traded in a certain period. A trader often calls this number the minimum trading volume. If you notice an increase in the volume, it denotes that other traders want that asset or stock. An increase in this volume will indicate that the price of the currency will go down or up very soon.

Regional Differences

Every market has different hurdles in it, and these hurdles are used to overcome any issues. You can also use these hurdles if you want to have some opportunities. A day trading strategy in one country will not work well in another country. For instance, some countries do not believe the news, and because of this the market does not react to the news. You also cannot expect the market in these countries to function the way you would expect them to.

It is critical to consider some regulations. Remember that not all strategies can be applied to all stocks. You need to follow certain rules for each trade you make, and it is important to research so you learn about any regulations. Ensure the regulations do not make it hard for you to implement your strategy. Bear in mind you are putting your hard-earned money in an online account, and you cannot afford to lose that money.

Different countries have different regulations and loopholes, which you can learn to increase your profits. If you are in the West but want to trade in the Philippines, you should do your homework to learn about their taxes. Ensure you have answers to all your questions, especially the following:

Can I pay this tax abroad, or should I pay it domestically?

What forms of tax do I have to pay?

Understand that any dissimilarity in the rates can change the profits made from trades.

Risk Management

Position size

You need to choose the position size that works for your capital and risk appetite. The position size is the shares you can buy in one trade. Calculate the difference between the stop-loss price and entry price to find the position size for yourself. For instance, if you want your stop-loss price to be $9.60 and the entry point price is $10, you can risk up to $0.40 per share. If you want to know the number of shares you can trade in one trade, divide the amount you are ready to invest by the risk price. This means you can take a position size of those many shares when you make one trade. Stick to this limit if you want to maintain your risk limit. It is also important to check if there is sufficient volume in the asset or stock you want to invest in, especially if you want to absorb the position size. Additionally, you must bear in mind that you will encounter slippage if you have a big position size in the market.

Stop-loss

Regardless of the type of strategy you choose, you need to consider the risk factor. It is important to do this to know you will never lose more than you can afford. If you are this way, you will be out of the game before you can do anything about it. Therefore, you need to set a stop-loss limit for yourself. The prices of stocks may seem like they are moving in the right direction, but this price can drop at any point. If you set up a stop-loss limit, you can control this risk. You can quit the trade and make a minimal loss on the security or asset if the price does not come through. Most traders, unfortunately, do not like to risk more than 1% of the capital they have set aside for trading. If there is $25,000 in your portfolio, you can only risk up to $250 on a single trade.

Best Cryptocurrencies to Day Trade

Cryptocurrencies are the greatest innovation in today's digital world. These currencies have gained immense popularity across the globe, and they work the way money works. At least they were designed to represent digital money. Cryptocurrencies are now looked at as substitutes to fiat currencies. Therefore, it is no surprise that people have started to trade cryptocurrencies in the market. Most people engage in trading cryptocurrencies depending on how much risk they can take.

People across the globe accept cryptocurrencies as a form of investment. The exchange of these currencies has improved over time, and it is critical to understand and talk about them. This section covers the best cryptocurrencies that you should consider when you use day trading as a strategy.

USDT or Tether

This cryptocurrency is only priced at one dollar, but it is considered one of the easiest and best cryptocurrencies to invest in. This happens due to various reasons. Tether has a huge volume that is used in trading. If you look at the numbers, you will notice that this cryptocurrency has the highest trading volume within a day. It is no wonder why this currency is critical when it comes to the cryptocurrency market. These trading volumes indicate that more traders will choose to invest in this cryptocurrency. The price of this currency does not go below $1, but it did happen a few weeks ago when the price fell below $1. Since the coin is stable when compared to other cryptocurrencies, it grabs the attention of a lot of day traders.

Ethereum

Ethereum is the next popular cryptocurrency after Bitcoin. It is for this reason that people invest in this currency as often as Bitcoin. Another reason why traders like this cryptocurrency is because this is also a blockchain. Using this blockchain platform, traders can create and develop decentralized applications. They can also generate tokens. In day trading, you have to always look for volatility. This is what helps traders make more profits. It is also essential to make sure the volatility is in a short period. Ethereum is now on most stock market exchanges, and it is easy for people to trade in this currency. The currency is presently priced at $3850.

BNB or Binance Coin

A decade ago, Binance, one of the well-known exchanges, released the Binance Coin, which is its own cryptocurrency. When this coin hit the market, traders noted it came from a reliable exchange, and they trusted the cryptocurrency. Traders also chose this cryptocurrency because of the demand for the currency. This currency is currently priced at $560, and it is a great way to begin day trading.

TRX or Tron

TRX or Tron is one currency that has garnered ample attention across the globe due to the developments made on this currency. This price, combined with the currency's high volatility, makes this one of the best currencies to trade in. The developers of Tron had initially used it to clear or remove any borders on the World Wide Web. They also wanted to ensure people could exchange content easily. Since the idea of the platform was valuable and gained a lot of traction, the currency is also growing steadily.

EOS

EOS is one cryptocurrency whose price has reached its maximum numerous times in a day. This indicates the volatility of this cryptocurrency. Therefore, when you trade this cryptocurrency, you can make profits, and sometimes these profits can be quite high. If you have the right knowledge or know a team that works on exchanging this cryptocurrency, you are good to go.

Cryptocurrency Trading Strategies

Cryptocurrencies are unpredictable, and this adds an exciting element when you choose to invest in them. Most day traders tend to look for different opportunities to make money, and the cryptocurrency market is the safest bet for them. If you choose to invest in the cryptocurrency market, you have to understand the price movement of the currencies. You don't need to purchase these coins and hold them for long. You can use the strategies mentioned above, as well as the ones mentioned in this section. It is easy to maximize your profits when you invest in cryptocurrencies since the market is volatile.

Breakout

If you choose this strategy, bear in mind that everything you do is going to rely on cryptocurrency. You can maintain a chart with different price levels, and you can use this strategy. You need to update this chart frequently to understand when the cryptocurrency stock has reached the volume you need it to, and the price has crossed the specific price level. Ensure you invest in this cryptocurrency immediately.

A trader using this strategy will enter the long position only when the stock's price increases above the specified price. If you choose to enter the market in a short position, ensure the volume of cryptocurrencies in the market matches the volume you are willing to invest in. If you trade in a currency above the criteria, the volatility of this currency will increase, and the price will move to the breakout. Ensure that you identify the right stock to trade in. If you do this, bear in mind your resistance levels and the support. You can invest in the currency if the points are frequently met.

Entry Points

It is easy for you to do this since you only have to set the following points:

The price is set close to the resistance level. This price will give you a bearish position.

The price is set close to the support level. This price will give you a bullish position.

Plan the Exits

It is significant to determine when you should exit any strategy. If you use chart patterns or moving average patterns, you need to look at the trend and assess it accurately. This allows you to calculate the price of the cryptocurrency and set the targets accordingly. If the price movement of the currency is 3 points above the previous price swings, you can invest in that stock. Once you reach this goal, you can plan the exits and reap the benefits.

Limiting Your Losses

It is extremely important to do this, especially if you trade within a certain margin. This margin is often quite high for a day trader, and when you trade within this margin, you are going to be vulnerable. If the price of the cryptocurrency changes, you are going to have trouble with the stock in the market. This means you will generate a high profit, but it also means you may incur significant losses if you are not careful about your limits. You can, however, employ a stop-loss limit to minimize these losses.

Stop-loss limits help you control and eliminate the risk. If you have a short position, place a stop-loss limit anywhere between a recent high or recent low of the price of the cryptocurrency. You can also do this basis your current risk portfolio. This limit is dependent on volatility. For instance, if a stock price changes by $0.1 every few seconds, place a stop-loss limit of $0.5 on the position. This helps you win regardless of which direction the currency moves in.

Traders often have two stop-loss limits. The first limit is a physical stop-loss limit they place. They believe they can lose this amount of money, which is known as the risk capital. The second limit they place is their mental stop loss which is where the strategy they use is no longer working for them - if you see that a position has made the wrong turn, exit immediately.

Reversal

This strategy is a potentially dangerous strategy for a beginner to use. It is a hotly debated strategy. Many traders worldwide use Reverse trading and is often termed as pull back trending, mean reversion strategy, and trend trading. In this strategy, you must only trade based on the trend and not based on any logic. You must accurately define the pullbacks and also predict the strengths of those pullbacks. To do this, you must have enough experience and very good knowledge of the market. An example of the reversal strategy is the daily pivot strategy. This strategy will focus on buying and selling stocks based on the high and low reverses or pullbacks.

Scalping

This is another common day trading strategy used for trading different types of stocks, including cryptocurrencies. This strategy is often used in the forex market, and a trader will use it to maximize profits on any small price changes. If you use scalping, you need to focus only on the quantity. If you wish to sell currencies the second they are equipped to be traded, use this strategy. It is an exciting way to trade but is extremely risky. You need to have a high trading probability and a very low risk-to-reward ratio. Ensure you track the market and look for any external factors that can influence the market that will make the price of the currency volatile. Follow the market to know when to sell your currencies. This is pretty much the only way you can make sure you don't suffer large losses.

Momentum

Beginners popularly use this strategy. In this strategy, the trader should focus only on news sources to identify any trends in the market. They should also identify those stocks whose prices change based on the news. There are always a few stocks that constantly move by twenty percent each day because of the news, so a trader can choose to invest in this stock. You should ensure that you hold your position and track the market. You should exit the position if you see any reversal. You can also fade on the price drop. You can do this when you see that the volume you want to invest in no longer exists. This is a simple strategy to use and is effective if you use it correctly. You should, however, ensure that you are aware of any news or earnings announcements. Make sure that you track your position regularly. A few seconds will also make a huge difference.

Moving Average Lines

Day trading strategies for cryptocurrencies rely only on the principles of day trading. Use the various strategies outlined in the sections above when trading in stocks. This section outlines the moving average crossover strategy that is often applied to the stock market. If you use stock trading strategies, you need to use the three moving average lines:

Set the first moving average line to twenty periods which will be the fastest moving average line in your strategy

The second is the slowest moving average line, and this should be set at sixty periods

The last average line should be 100 periods which will help you identify the trend in the trade

This type of strategy often sends you signals and indicators for purchasing any stock in the market. Bear in mind that these lines need to be tracked closely, especially when the fastest line intersects with the slowest line. If this happens, it is an indication that you have to sell the cryptocurrency. This signal will tell you when the fastest moving average line will go below the slowest moving average line. This way, you open a position for yourself when the line crosses in one direction. The position closes only when the lines move in the opposite way. It is easy for you to identify this trend if the price bar is above the third line. You can learn more about the moving average technique if you want to only trade in stocks.

Spread Betting Strategies

Spread betting strategies often allow you to speculate on how to trade on global markets. There is no need to own any currency or asset on this market since the strategy is relatively straightforward. You can learn these strategies on different news pages and websites.

CFD Strategies

It is difficult for most traders to come up with a trading strategy that works for them and helps them maximize profits. Most strategies are often complex to implement. You can always opt for an instrument like CFD to make your job easier. CFD strategies are only focused on the difference in the price of entering and exiting that trade. You can easily make a profit on the underlying asset on which you are trading without owning the asset. The one thing you have to understand is know how the asset moves.

Using Pivot Points

If you are a beginner, it is best to use the pivot point strategy only when you know how to perform technical analysis. This strategy will help you identify or act on some resistance or support levels that are critical to your position. This is a useful strategy to use in the forex market. You can also use this method if you are interested in trading out of your bounds. It is best to identify your entry points in the market. You can use a trend or breakout to assess these points. If the value of the exchange falls in this range, you will make a profit.

Calculating Pivot Points

Have you heard Ross Geller yell "Pivot" when he was trying to move his couch on the staircase? That's a pivot. It is the point that can allow you to rotate. You can use the historical information to calculate the pivot points. As a day trader, use the previous day's price fluctuation and the final price of that stock for the day and calculate the pivot point. Understand that the accuracy of the point will continue to reduce if you use short-term prices since these prices are not a good indicator of the cryptocurrency price. Use the following formula to calculate the pivot point:

Central Pivot Point (P) = (High + Low + Close)/3

When you calculate this value, you can use it to calculate your resistance levels. Use the following formulae to do this:

First Support (S1) = (2 * P) – High

First Resistance (R1) = (2 * P) – Low

You can then calculate the second levels using the following formulae:

Second Support (S2) = P – (R1 – S1)

Second Resistance (R1) = P + (R1 − S1)

Application

If you apply this method to the cryptocurrency market, you see the trading range in every session is going to be within the pivot points you set. There is going to be a resistance and a support level. Many traders choose to play only within this range because it is a safer bet. It is important to understand that you can apply this method to stock index prices too. For example, you can use this method to develop any other strategy that will help you maximize profits in the cryptocurrency trade market.

Forex Trading Strategies

It is difficult to trade in this market, but most cryptocurrencies are traded in the forex market. The only disadvantage of this trading strategy is that you must accumulate your profits and limit your losses quickly. You can use any of the trading strategies mentioned earlier in this chapter, but it is important to learn some strategies used in the forex market so you are not in the blind when something new hits the market.

Tips

Now that you have an idea about day trading and which currencies you should trade in let us look at some tips to help you make the right choices when you invest and trade in cryptocurrencies.

Do Your Due Diligence

As mentioned earlier, you must have the right knowledge about day trading. Additionally, you need to learn the basic processes and procedures while you learn about the stock market. It is also important for you to follow the news. Keep an eye out for any event that may affect the price of stocks, like the economic outlook, the interest rate plans, etc. Ensure you learn about the stock. Make the list of stocks you wish to trade in so you arc informed about the status of companies. You can also learn how well the company is doing and continue investing in it. Visit the right websites so you have the correct information about the company.

Set Some Money Aside

Assess your financial situation and know how much capital you can risk when you trade in the market. Many investors who use day trading are willing to risk at most two percent of their funds when they invest. Let us assume that you have $40,000 in your account, and you can afford to lose 0.5% of the capital on each trade. The maximum loss that you can make per trade is $40,000 * 0.05 = $200. Set aside some money or funding, so you can use it in case you make any losses. Remember that this is just a fund you can use in emergency situations.

Set Some Time Aside for Trading

It is essential to spend ample time on day trading. This process is called day trading for a specific reason. Spend some time during the day looking at the market and understanding what you can invest in. Never choose this option as your career if you do not have too much time to spare. Spot the right opportunities, look for the right events, and track every stock on the market, which will lead to some changes in the stock market. Bear in mind that you move through the process quickly.

Start Small

If you are new to the stock market, especially new to investing in cryptocurrencies, then start small. Focus on two stocks every session. When you do this, you can study the market and identify when you should invest in the stock. If you look at multiple stocks at once, you are going to make mistakes. Trace the market and spot the right opportunities if you just have a few stocks to look at. Most people trade just a small portion of the share they earn. So, this means you can specify smaller dollar amounts. This should be the amount you must invest. For instance, if Microsoft shares are traded at $100 in the market, and you only want to shell out $10 from your account, then purchase only $1/10^{th}$ of the shares you are interested in.

Do Not Use Penny Stocks

Most traders look for stocks that have low prices, and penny stocks are one such type. It is important to stay away from these stocks since they are illiquid. This means you cannot make a huge profit on these stocks. A penny stock is often traded as low as $5 and sometimes lower. Penny stocks can only be traded OTC and aren't placed on the stock market. It is best to invest in these stocks only if you have done your due diligence and see that you can make a profit. Otherwise, steer clear of them.

Time Your Trades

Most investors and traders make their trades when the market opens. This adds a certain level of volatility in the prices. If you are an experienced investor or trader, it becomes easy for you to identify these patterns in the prices and pick the right stocks to invest in, thereby making a profit. As a beginner, you must learn about the market before you purchase a stock. Never make a move until twenty minutes after the market opens. The prices fluctuate for the first few hours. It is only during the afternoon that the prices are relatively stable, but they will continue to fluctuate nearing the close of the market, as well. The rush hours are where you can make profits, but it is a good practice for beginners to avoid these.

If You Want to Cut Losses, Use Limit Orders

Decide on the type of order you wish to use when you enter or exit any cryptocurrency or trade. Ensure you know if you should use market orders or limit orders. If you want to place a market order, remember the order is only executed when the trade you want to make is at its best price. Bear in mind the price is not a guarantee. On the other hand, a limit order will guarantee the price but not the execution of the market. A limit order helps you trade with precision. It lets you set your price. Ensure the price you set is executable and not unrealistic. This price is for both buying and selling stock. Sophisticated and experienced day traders often use the same methods because they know they work for them. This helps them maintain their positions and hedge their bets.

Be Realistic About the Profits You Make

You should understand that your strategy doesn't have to be right only if you make profits. Bear in mind that you will only make a 60% profit in most cases as a trader. While you will lose some of the money you have invested, it is best to compare the amount of money you have lost against the amount gained. This lets you decide if the strategy you have employed is good for you. Ensure that the risk against each of your strategies is limited to a specific amount. It is important to define the entry and exit methods for your trades.

Stay Calm

There are bound to be times when the market will test your nerves. The prices may not move the way you want them to. In such cases, learn to maintain a level head. Understand that you cannot control the market, and there is only so much you can do to make profits. Let go of your emotions and stop using them to make decisions about where you want to invest. Only decide based on logic.

Write a Plan and Abide By It

To be successful, you have to move fast. That doesn't mean you have to think fast. That's because every successful trader has the right strategies in mind and knows he should be disciplined and stay true to his plan. It is important you always follow the formula closely and never chase your profits. Do not let your emotions get in the way because they will only make it harder for you to do well. Do not, under any circumstances, abandon your strategy. You should follow the mantra *"Plan your trade and trade your plan."*

With these tips in hand and the different strategies you can use, you can step into the world of cryptocurrency day trading. Stick to your plan at every step but ensure you have the right plan in mind.

Chapter Eight: Trading Cryptocurrencies

Bitcoin Trading

Bitcoin trading speculates on movements in the cryptocurrency's price. Traditionally, this involved buying Bitcoin using a medium called exchanges and hoping that its value will surge in time. But now, traders are starting to use derivatives to speculate on rising and falling prices, to make most of Bitcoin's quality as a volatile currency,

With various online markets available, you can trade on the price of Bitcoin with commercial derivatives such as CFDs. This allows you to speculate on the currency's price movements or, more specifically, Bitcoin's price movements in either direction without owning the actual cryptocurrency. It means you don't get ownership of Bitcoin. Instead, you are opening a position that will increase or decrease in value, and this depends on Bitcoin's price movement against the dollar.

Bitcoin has guided the direction of most cryptocurrencies. It is the most common currency known to people who are new to the trading industry. Due to its volatility, traders can experience huge shifts in the price, which is why it has an appeal but risk too.

Steps Involved in Trading Bitcoin

Learn What Influences Bitcoin's Price

In order to find a great pricing prospect, you must learn about the characteristics that have an effect on Bitcoin's price:

Bitcoin Supply

The current Bitcoin quantity is topped at 21 million. This supply is expected to last at least until 2140. A limited supply means that if the demand for Bitcoin increases in the future, its price could also register a sharp rise.

Bad Press

Any news covered by media channels that is related to Bitcoin's safety, value, and durability will have a damaging impact on the coin's market value as it will harsh its reputation among new traders and investors.

Integration

Bitcoin's assimilation into the banking structures and new payment systems will affect its public profile. If it is carried out successfully and Bitcoin gets integrated with the payment systems, it could lead to a rise in demand and have a positive bearing on its price.

Key Events

Security violations, directive changes, and macroeconomic announcements, etc., can have an effect on Bitcoin prices. Agreements to speed up the network between users could also help push the price higher.

Pick a Bitcoin Trading Style and Plan

Day Trading

If you want to day trade Bitcoin, you will have to start and end a trade within a single trading day. Day trading implies that you would not have an overnight Bitcoin market exposure, and also the overnight funding charges will not have an impact on your position. If you are looking to earn profits from Bitcoin's short-term movements, you can choose this strategy of trading. It can give you a chance to make the best out of the coin's daily volatility. Day trading is maybe the best option for traders who are looking to create and grow a career in trading markets. It can be very technical and also takes a long time. Those who have the focus and dedication to analyze the charts regularly, day trading the simplest way to start investing in Bitcoin.

Trend Trading

Taking a position that matches the current trend is known as trend trading. For example, a trader who is using a trend trading strategy will go long when the market shows a bullish trend. When the trend shows a bearish slump, they will go short. They would close their position and open a new trade to match the new trend if the current trend starts to slow or goes in reverse. Unlike day trading, positions in trend trading can be held for a few days to a couple of weeks.

Bitcoin Hedging Strategy

The task of reducing your risk exposure by assuming a contrasting position to your current position is known as hedging Bitcoin. If you were anxious that the market would move against you, the hedging strategy is the one you should take. For instance, if a short-term drop in the value of your Bitcoins bothers you, you can opt for a short position on Bitcoin with Contracts for Difference or CFDs. If the market value of Bitcoin falls as you had expected, with the hedging strategy, the gains on your short position will cover most of the losses you incurred on your coins.

HODL Bitcoin Strategy

'Hodl' is just an investment philosophy. As per this strategy, you buy and hold Bitcoin. It got its name from an error in the spell for the word 'hold' on a famous crypto forum. It now stands for "hold on to dear life." It suggests that the best

Bitcoin investment strategy is to hold it forever. The phrase should not be taken too seriously, though. You must 'buy and hold' Bitcoin only if you get a positive perspective on its long-term value. If you feel otherwise, and if trading plans suggest you sell your position for a profit or to limit your loss, you must do it.

Get Exposure to Bitcoin

Trading Bitcoin Derivatives

Trading Bitcoin derivatives implies that you will speculate on its value with Contracts for Differences (CFDs) rather than outrightly owning Bitcoin.

Buying Bitcoin through an Exchange

The most popular way to buy Bitcoin is to go through an online exchange directly. These exchanges are the middlemen of cryptocurrency investing, like a stock brokerage. Traders who have a buy-and-hold strategy are the ones who mostly buy Bitcoin through an exchange. This is mainly because buying from an exchange means you get ownership of the Bitcoin because you expect that there will be a rise in its price.

If you decide to purchase from an exchange, you will have to select from an assortment of options. Here are a few of the most popular exchanges:

Coinbase

This is the most accepted cryptocurrency exchange across the world. It insures against losses and provides security against any fraudulent transfers.

Bitfinex

Seattle-based Bitfinex is the oldest cryptocurrency exchange. It is suited for advanced traders, investors, and lenders. Bitfinex charges an "inactivity fee" if you don't trade on your account and hold your balances in the account.

Gemini

This New York-based cryptocurrency exchange has high regulatory standards. When you purchase Bitcoin through an exchange, it is stored in a "wallet." It is a software program that helps you manage your digital currency. They have two kinds of wallets:

Hot wallet

Your Bitcoin exchange operates a hot wallet. Some exchanges instantly provide you with a hot wallet when you open your account with them. Since you can access your coins through the Internet or a software program, hot wallets are convenient. Some examples of hot wallets are:

Electrum - This software helps you to store your coins on your computer.

Mycelium - This wallet is a mobile-only app for Android and iPhone users.

However easy to use, hot wallets are not the most secure form of coin storage. If the hot wallet provider were hacked, then your coin information would be at risk.

Cold wallet

A cold wallet is an actual piece of hardware that stores your coins. It is usually a portable device that is similar to a flash drive. A cold wallet might cost you around $60 to $100. Some popular cold wallets are:

Trezor

Ledger Nano

A cold wallet is the safest storage method to store your coins. If you are trading high amounts of coins, then you must invest in a cold wallet.

Although a popular choice, there are a few problems with buying Bitcoin using an exchange:

Oftentimes, the exchanges don't have the proper guidelines and infrastructure required to respond speedily to support requirements.

The market can be suspended, or there is reduced execution correctness due to the identical servers and engines on many Bitcoin exchanges are unreliable.

Bitcoin exchanges regularly levy fees and some forms of limitations on funding as well as on withdrawing from the exchange.

Since there are certain risks involved in using exchanges, here are some factors you should go through before choosing an exchange:

Security

This is a critical issue in the crypto industry since exchanges are at constant risk of frauds, hacks, and pump-and-dump schemes. Therefore, it is important to research your exchange before choosing them. Online reviews in different forums or on sites like Reddit is one way to help you choose a safe and secure platform for your investment.

Liquidity

If there is insufficient liquidity, the prices and the speed of your transactions will be compromised. Before you decide to purchase Bitcoin, make sure the exchange you have chosen offers sufficient liquidity and trading volume so as to ensure fast and easy transactions.

Ease of Use

This factor is very important to consider, especially for those who are new to the trading industry. You want your Bitcoin exchange to provide you with an easy-to-use interface.

Method of Payment

Always make sure that you check into the methods of payment the exchange accepts. Some Bitcoin exchanges require you to make deposits by bank transfer, some use PayPal, and some accept credit and debit card payments. Generally, the easier it is for you to pay, the more fees you will be charged because the exchanges will make you pay for the convenience.

Crypto 10 Index

Apart from trading Bitcoin byproducts or purchasing coins from exchanges, you can trade on the Crypto 10 Index. It offers you access to the ten best cryptocurrencies in a single trade.

Long or Short Trading

If, instead of using exchanges to buy your Bitcoin, you decide to trade financial derivatives, you can go long as well as short. If you assume that the Bitcoin price will rise, you can opt for long. Contrastingly, if you think that the price will fall, you can opt for short.

Stops and Limits Assignment

Stops and limits are important tools in risk management. There are generally a few options, they are:

Normal stops to stop your trade at an already decided level.

Trailing stops follow favorable market trends to earn profits. They cap your downside risk.

Guaranteed stops stop your trade at a level you set.

Check Your Trade

You would buy Bitcoin if the market trend predicted a rise in its value and sell if the trend predicted a decline in its value. When your trade opens, monitor and scan the market to ensure your trade is moving where you want it to so that you get a potential profit.

Cut Your Losses

While trading Bitcoin, you can shut your position at any time during the trade. You have the option of exiting at any point so you can profit, cut your losses and prevent further damage.

Tips for Investing in Bitcoin

Before you decide to invest in Bitcoin, here are some factors you should consider.

Start Out Small

When you start trading in Bitcoin, start out with a small investment and proceed with caution. Although it is an exciting market with a reputation for making people earn substantial profits in a short time, trading in Bitcoins is not easy, and there are risks involved.

Research the Market

Before investing your money, get to know the Bitcoin market. It is not easy, as many practices used to analyze other financial markets do not apply to Bitcoin. The effects of global events on the coin's value are highly unpredictable.

Understand Your Risk Tolerance

Bitcoin is a high-risk investment. It is extremely volatile too. You must check how much risk you can tolerate before you invest in Bitcoin. If you are not comfortable with volatile assets or do not have enough capital to invest, you may want to reconsider your decision to trade in Bitcoin. Do not invest more than you can afford to lose.

Be Strict With Profit Targets and Stop-Loss Orders

As mentioned earlier, Bitcoin is highly volatile, so it is crucial that you make a plan and follow it no matter what. Before you open a position, consider the level of profit that would satisfy you and what losses you can afford. Set your target stop-loss right from the beginning. Without a disciplined approach, it is easy to expose yourself to potentially destructive movements.

Buy and Hold Bitcoin

Buy and hold is a type of Bitcoin trading strategy. This is a passive approach strategy where traders hold positions anywhere from weeks to years. There are many benefits to this strategy:

Buying and holding Bitcoin allows the customers to bypass the currency's short-term volatility. Significant movement in the positions throughout any given day at the market is not an unusual sight in the crypto market. This signifies that a trader's stop loss and take profit targets are effortlessly achieved, throwing a person out of their trade.

Leverage Utility with Caution

Leverage is highly beneficial for traders. It enables them to hold a much higher stake in a trade than their actual capital limitations, opening a window for more transactions. Although leverage has its own share of charms, allowing people to make high rates of profits, it comes with its own cons. It can direct a trader from profits to huge amounts of losses.

Using leverage to work for your benefits requires experience and expertise. It is a balancing act between risk and reward and takes lots of effort and practice to master.

Controlled Emotions

Though risk management and strategy are the major deciding factors in Bitcoin trading success, there are other factors too you should be aware of. Emotional factors such as FOMO- fear of missing out is one such notable factor that can amply affect the success rate.

Everyone would agree that Bitcoin is a volatile feature, and too many dramatic price fluctuations in a short span aren't unusual. During an upward trend, a lot of traders face FOMO, fearing that they might miss major profits if they don't get into the action soon. The failure to resist this temptation might result in a series of other failures.

Buying during an upward trend goes against the most basic rule of trading- buy low, sell high. Now, let's say the trader buys during the upward trend. This indicates that he has already missed the beneficial point of the upward trend, as now it is inevitable that price will go low and the trader will end up paying a premium for an asset, placing them at a significant loss.

Ethereum Trading

How to Buy Ethereum?

Cryptocurrency exchanges are the most common way of acquiring Ethereum. These exchanges provide a variety of options for purchasing and selling Ethereum to its users. For example, exchanges such as OKEx give margin, decentralized or spot trading, whereas other options such as BitMex offer a mix of spot trading and person-to-person trading. Other options like Coinbase are also available if one wants to trade their fiat currency directly to purchase Ethereum. In fact, LocalBitcoins allows investors to purchase Bitcoin in pretty much any currency across the world.

Some of the most popular and widely used cryptocurrency platforms and exchanges are:

Kraken

This crypto exchange is available for traders at all levels, providing dozens of options to choose from. Kraken offers spot trading to investors. It also gives crypto derivatives to its users as a part of the package. Around 150+ trade and more than 30 coins are available at this exchange.

Gemini

Gemini is a crypto spot exchange. More than 40 trade pairs and 20+ coins are available at GEMINI. It is crypto storage regulated under NYSTC, and it provides ample amounts of learning material to its users.

Bitflex

This is a crypto exchange with perpetuals, futures, and five times leverage on the selected derivatives. BITFINEX has dozens of coins available and a lot of trade pairs on its site.

Huobi

With around 200+ coins and around 500+ trade pairs, Huobi is a top-rated choice for customers. This crypto exchange has five times the leverage for spot trading, futures, and swap. It also offers the chance for customer-to-customer lending.

Binance

BINANCE is a top-rated exchange with hundreds of coins, futures, and leveraged tokens. It has 600+ trade pairs. Also, BINANCE provides crypto loans to its users.

BlockFi

Here, investors and traders can buy and sell major cryptocurrencies like Ethereum and Bitcoin. BlockFi is also an option for traders who want to trade altcoins like PAXG and stablecoin. 10+ trade pairs and coins are accessible on BlockFi.

OKEX

OKEX is a crypto exchange for spot trading, futures, perpetual swap, and derivatives trading. OKEX has 300+ trade pairs and 100+ coins on its platform and offers access to hot and cold wallets too.

StormGain

A crypto exchange that charges very low fees from its customers and provides a 200 times multiplier on crypto futures. 10+ trade pairs and coins are accessible on StormGain.

Where to Buy Ethereum?

Not everyone buys Ethereum. Instead of purchasing Ethereum, they use an alternative of trading Ethereum byproducts such as CFDs (Contract for Difference) and forex using a broker.

Trading through a broker has its own advantages. A broker permits an investor to gain benefits from changes in prices of Ethereum without owning a piece of this currency in reality.

CFDs are a very complex tool, and they always come with a very high risk of losing money quickly due to the presence of leverage. More than 60% of retail investors have accounted for losing money while trading CFDs instruments. One should analyze their position and then make a calculated decision. An investor should consider various points before arriving at a decision - whether they fully understand how CFDs work, do they possess enough capital to risk their money, etc.

Why Should One Trade Ethereum?

There are many reasons for doing so, few of them are:

First Mover Advantage & Network Effect

It is a computational machine that permits smart contracts, unlike other cryptos. It is a first-of-its-kind machine. In the Ethereum network, many smart contracts and network development have happened before any other cryptocurrencies. A lot of newer networks try to compete with Ethereum in the same sphere, but their efforts have been futile so far. Until and unless they transform quicker than Ethereum, they won't be able to win the race with Ethereum.

Mainstream Corporate Acceptance

Ethereum, with its huge innovation capabilities, has drawn the attention of major established corporations and tech giants like Cisco, Microsoft, and Intel. Ethereum's network is highly decentralized, and it allows a lot more computational operations than just being a payment network for its users.

In fact, the tech giant Microsoft has come up with its own Ethereum based platform named Coco, which they are offering to their clients. This option has been created for the companies that seek alternative database structures so that they can take full benefit of major blockchain strengths.

Robust Development Team

The main focus of Ethereum is building a democratized and decentralized computing machine. Its vision is more extensive than other cryptocurrencies. Cryptos such as Bitcoin and Monero have a narrow focus on securing and scaling the market. Ethereum's project is much grander than these platforms. The developers at Ethereum are highly interested in innovation and keep trying to find out what new things the Ethereum network can accomplish and how they make these projects a success.

Such flexibility with ideas attracts developers who themselves have a diverse range of abilities making Ethereum a more original device than the rest of the networks.

Though Ethereum provides many incentives to its users, it has its share of cons.

Why Should One Not Trade Ethereum?

A crypto world would look very promising to an infant investor, but one should always gather all kinds of information and seek professional guidance before making any investment decisions.

Network Congestion Issues

Enhanced and standard computational competency and smart abilities make Ethereum a popular platform among investors in the field of blockchain technology. Ethereum works great when it comes to making a choice for most ICOs (Initial Coin Offerings) that use this network, not just for their coin and token sales. A lot of major projects use the smart contracts on the Ethereum network for their functionality.

The potential of token sales alone has contributed to the major success of Ethereum's network and has easily stretched it to its capacity. At the peak of the network, a fun hack-a-thon project called the CryptoKitties was launched to the network, and it was solely adequate to take the network to unimaginable and extraordinary congestion.

Large Attack Surface

Bitcoin's programming is limited to simply computing very low level and simple financial functions. On the other hand, Ethereum's programming is a lot more functional. It is easily adept at performing the calculations needed to perform smart contracts.

The very complex nature of Ethereum has become a bane for the network. With high complications comes a bigger attack surface, increasing the security issues for the network. In simple words, it means a lot can go wrong if there are too many elements.

Network's smart contracts for the users are far from foolproof, which produces a major risk. As per reports, some well-planned and thought-out peer-reviewed contracts have either failed or have been hacked. Investors and traders that have high capital potential and financial backups should have a strong foothold in the Ethereum market.

Proof of Stake Uncertainty

Like Bitcoin, Ethereum also currently utilizes PoW (Proof of Work) to procure proof of the legitimacy of the transactions on its blockchain network. But, in recent times, Proof of Work has received huge criticism for being a very inept and incompetent use of the resources for offering the service it does.

As a result, Ethereum has decided to transition to PoS (Proof of Stake), providing the stakeholders the option of being the final arbiters of the state of the network and not miners. Ethereum is also trying to change this essential blockchain alteration "in-flight" on the live blockchain, which can lead to heavy network "turbulence."

Therefore, investors should look at both- the pros and cons of crypto technology and then make a final decision, or there is a huge possibility of large capital losses.

LiteCoin Trading

LiteCoin (LTC) can be called silver if you consider Bitcoin to be gold. Silver is usually unpredictable as compared to gold, which makes LiteCoin an interesting prospect for traders.

How Does LiteCoin Work?

LiteCoin is different from Bitcoin in a few but significant ways.

LiteCoin can be mined faster than Bitcoin. The average block is approved and added to the blockchain in less than three minutes. Bitcoin takes around ten minutes, which makes LiteCoin transactions and transfers faster.

The supply of LiteCoin is capped at 84 million, which is four times the supply of Bitcoin.

What Affects LiteCoin's Price?

Given that its qualities are very similar to Bitcoin, it isn't a revelation that the components influencing LiteCoin's price are similar to those for Bitcoin.

LiteCoin Supply

Several people point out that LiteCoin has a broader supply, and because of that, it has a lower price than Bitcoin. Regardless of the fact that it launched after two years, there is way too much accessibility of LiteCoins in the market. LiteCoin's transactions are faster, too, which ensures that the supply stays fluid.

Bad Press

Media coverage of negative news regarding LiteCoin or cryptocurrencies in common can massively affect the coin's value. LiteCoin's value is totally based on how the public perceives the digital currency, which renders it additionally dependent on favorable news headlines.

Industry Adoption

The insistence that LiteCoin possesses several advantages over Bitcoin will remain unconfirmed until it starts being accepted as a valid mode of payment by corporations around the world. So a prominent institution adopting this currency could spike its value in the market.

LTC Market Cap

Since investors who buy and hold the cryptocurrency are a major reason for LiteCoin's price rises, they will be attentive towards the trade and market cap just as soon as they realize that they have to make a decision if they should acquire more or sell.

Bitcoin's Price

LiteCoin follows Bitcoin, and therefore changes in Bitcoin's prices can affect its value.

How to Buy LiteCoin?

Use an Exchange

One way to own LiteCoin is through a cryptocurrency exchange. Here are a few popular exchanges you can use:

Coinbase

It is probably the best and simplest way to buy LiteCoins using a credit card or a bank transfer.

Coinmama

This exchange lately augmented the ability to acquire LiteCoin with USD promptly on the platform. Investors or traders from almost any nation in the world can utilize this platform to purchase LiteCoins with US dollars or other FIAT currencies such as GBP. Coinmama is one of the best limits providing exchanges.

Binance

It is one of the largest cryptocurrency exchanges across the globe. Binance supports bank and card purchases.

Risks of Exchanges

If you decide to trade in LiteCoin, you need to be sure that the exchange you are using is secure. Always enable two-factor authorization and do not keep all your coins in a single wallet. You also need to be extra careful with your wallet's access codes or keys.

Your Trading Plan

A thorough plan would be a good place to start if you decide to trade in LiteCoin. Here are some steps you can observe to come up with the perfect plan for your trade:

Be clear with your trading objectives, define them concisely and divide them into short-term and long-term goals.

If you are not sticking only to LiteCoin, decide the markets you should trade in.

Set up your risk-reward ratio. Choose the level of risk you can tolerate, one that does not make you uncomfortable.

Keep a trading journal to note down what works and what does not.

Study all the trading strategies and carefully choose which one you would prefer to apply.

Work Out Your Analysis

You should ensure that you know of the latest improvements in the LiteCoin market before you open your first position.

Plan your first trade carefully. You may want to contemplate carrying out some technical evaluation on LiteCoin.

Trading in Leveraged LiteCoin

Purchasing LiteCoin CFDs (Contract for Differences) may bear some resemblance to buying LTC on an exchange. The position of the investor will increase in value as LTCs price rises. It usually increases against the US Dollar. Though there is a slight resemblance, there are several major differences as well.

First of all, when an investor opens a leveraged LiteCoin trade, in reality, they don't own the cryptocurrency. They are not availing any kind of ownership. Instead of that, the investor is just heading and speculating in the direction in which its price is headed. This means that a trader can open short as well as long positions, anything of their own choice, without needing any sort of exchange account.

The second point is that the trader does not require paying or putting down the full value of a leveraged LiteCoin position upfront - he can just make a simple small deposit known as 'margin.' Though this might look like an advantage of using LiteCoin making leveraged trading a powerful tool for the customers, it actually makes it a bit riskier. Supposing that the trader's position moves against them, they can actually lose a bigger amount than their initial original deposit.

Conclusion

You now have a clear idea about the basics of investing in cryptocurrencies. You also know exactly what to expect and how not to think when you invest in them. Using this information, you can now begin investing in the right currencies and choosing the right strategies to invest in.

I hope the information in this book helps you make an educated decision when you invest in cryptocurrencies. This book has everything there is that needs to know about cryptocurrencies, how to trade in them, the different strategies you can use, and so much more. You will learn everything there is to trading in these currencies before you throw your money into the market.

The objective of the book is to give you an understanding of cryptocurrency and how you can invest in it. The book also has given you a brief of various exchange platforms and blockchain. The book also has a lot of information about different strategies. As mentioned earlier, the book will only give you a tour of the cryptocurrency world, but you need to do your due diligence and research before you trade in any currency as an investor. Understand the mechanism and technology that oils the cryptocurrency market. Follow trends and research as much as you can before making any investment. Diversifying is key and has been mentioned in several chapters of this book.

Do not put all your money into investing in cryptocurrencies because that can lead to failure. Diversification is key, and if you are unsure of what to do, reach out to a consultant or broker to help you. While it may be interesting and adventurous to invest alone, do it only if you are certain of what you are investing in. Bear in mind that you won't be making profits every time. You are bound to make losses, but you can write off these losses if you set up your investment structure the right way. This can only happen when you have enough risk capital.

Understand the risks of investing in cryptocurrencies and be ready to make mistakes. Experts suggest that you test your strategies and try learning through different platforms, such as Investopedia, which will view how the market works. It is best to practice and test your strategies before you apply them in the real world. Bear in mind that all your strategies may not work in all cases.

I hope this book was useful and has answered a lot of your questions about cryptocurrency. I wish you luck in your endeavors of investment and carrying out your first-ever cryptocurrency portfolio tailored to your needs and risk appetite.

Resources

CoinDCX. (2020, October 27). Tips & tricks to maximize returns on your crypto investments. Retrieved from Coindcx.com website: https://blog.coindcx.com/tips-and-tricks-to-maximize-returns-on-your-cryptocurrency-investments/

Cudd, M., Ritterbush, K., Eduardo, M., & Smith, C. (2019). Cryptocurrency Returns. In A. Salman & M. G. A. Razzaq (Eds.), *Blockchain and Cryptocurrencies*. London, England: IntechOpen.

Editor, E. B. R. (2020, July 14). Advantages of cryptocurrency: All you need to know. Retrieved from Europeanbusinessreview.com website: https://www.europeanbusinessreview.com/advantages-of-cryptocurrency-all-you-need-to-know/

Folger, J. (2021, May 13). Top 10 rules for successful trading. Retrieved from Investopedia.com website: https://www.investopedia.com/articles/trading/10/top-ten-rules-for-trading.asp

Frankenfield, J. (2021, May 21). HODL. Retrieved from Investopedia.com website: https://www.investopedia.com/terms/h/hodl.asp

Huffman, E. (2021, June 3). Best cryptocurrencies in 2021. Retrieved from Benzinga.com website: https://www.benzinga.com/money/best-cryptocurrency/

Jack, P. (2020, July 11). Crypto trading vs Stock trading: Which is more profitable in 2021? Retrieved from The Capital website: https://medium.com/the-capital/crypto-trading-vs-stock-trading-which-is-more-profitable-in-2020-554dc1a58b30

Laura, M. (2020, November 4). Cryptocurrency trading: Everything you need to know in 2021. Retrieved from Bitdegree.org website: https://www.bitdegree.org/crypto/tutorials/cryptocurrency-trading

Levy, A. (2020, November 13). Is Cryptocurrency a Good Investment? Retrieved from Fool.com website: https://www.fool.com/investing/stock-market/market-sectors/financials/blockchain-stocks/is-cryptocurrency-good-investment/

Mazer, J. (2017, August 24). Demystifying Cryptocurrencies, Blockchain, and ICOs. Retrieved from Toptal.com website: https://www.toptal.com/finance/market-research-analysts/cryptocurrency-market

McNamara, R., Co-President, & Blockchain, W. (2021, February 18). How to trade cryptocurrency. Retrieved from Benzinga.com website: https://www.benzinga.com/money/how-to-trade-cryptocurrency/

Polly. (2020, September 16). Tips on how to choose which cryptocurrency to trade. Retrieved from Roboticsandautomationnews.com website: https://roboticsandautomationnews.com/2020/09/16/tips-on-how-to-choose-which-cryptocurrency-to-trade/36487/

Reiff, N. (2020, September 12). Investing in cryptocurrencies: What to keep in mind. Retrieved from Investopedia.com website: https://www.investopedia.com/news/investing-cryptocurrencies-what-keep-mind/

Top cryptocurrency exchanges Ranked by volume. (n.d.). Retrieved from Coinmarketcap.com website: https://coinmarketcap.com/rankings/exchanges/

What are the risks? (2021, May 18). Retrieved from Cmcmarkets.com website: https://www.cmcmarkets.com/en/learn-cryptocurrencies/what-are-the-risks

(2018). *Buying vs trading cryptocurrencies_Website+*. IG.

(N.d.). Retrieved from Forbes.com website: https://www.forbes.com/sites/investor/2020/05/12/3-traps-to-avoid-when-trading-Bitcoin-and-crypto/?sh=65ead0b666a7